IROQUOIS

MAYA

INCA

INDIANS

of the

AMERICAS

HISTORICAL PAGEANT

Since 1917, first as Director of the Rockefeller Foundation and later as President of the Julius Rosenwald Fund, Edwin Rogers Embree has given himself to studies of race, culture, education, and public health. During this time he has visited for considerable periods seventeen countries of Europe, nine of Asia, and nine of Oceanica, as well as all Central American states. His best-known book is a study of the American negro, 'Brown America: The Story of a New Race.'

BOOKS BY EDWIN R. EMBREE

ILLUSTRATIONS BY HOWARD GRIEG

INDIANS *of*

the AMERICAS

HISTORICAL PAGEANT

EDWIN R. EMBREE

BOSTON

HOUGHTON MIFFLIN COMPANY

𝕿𝖍𝖊 𝕽𝖎𝖛𝖊𝖗𝖘𝖎𝖉𝖊 𝕻𝖗𝖊𝖘𝖘 𝕮𝖆𝖒𝖇𝖗𝖎𝖉𝖌𝖊
1939

The Riverside Press

CAMBRIDGE · MASSACHUSETTS

PRINTED IN THE U.S.A.

CONTENTS

ILLUSTRATIONS

Strange canoes with great white wings

PROLOGUE

WHITE MAGIC

ON A SUNNY AUTUMN DAY in the year that we know as 1492, a group of Indians on a little island of the western tropics suddenly stopped gathering in their harvest and ran down to the shore. They pointed in wild excitement at the sea, for riding on the waters toward them were three strange canoes with great white wings. Swiftly the huge birds came to the island, and out of them poured men the like of whom had never been seen. They had pale skins; they had long hair growing from their faces; they wore queer, heavy clothes; their talk was gibberish.

The Indians were so filled with curiosity and surprise that they almost forgot their manners. But mustering some calm and dignity, the chief made a speech of welcome while the people began to prepare a feast and gather presents to show their friendship. It was clear that the visitors were excited too. They chattered among themselves in their strange tongue; they stared; they shouted; they fell upon their knees and lifted their white faces to the sky.

The new beings were not only strange — they were rude and greedy. They grabbed the presents which the Indians offered. They fell upon the food without waiting for their hosts to join them. They shouted and struck the red men when they did not understand. The islanders drew away in fear and the palefaces raised strange war clubs to their shoulders, clubs that bellowed, spit fire, and hurled magic balls which tore through the flesh more fiercely than any arrow. And the Indians thought such powerful magic could belong only to gods.

Baffled, awed by the grotesque, godlike appearance of the strangers, terrified by the magic war clubs and the brutal manners, the frightened Indians continued to serve their guests. But courtesies were answered by gruff shouts; offers of presents simply drove the strangers to hunting for more treasure which they seized without the asking.

As the days passed, the visitors sailed on to near-by islands, and everywhere the suffering of the Indians grew. Many times the war clubs thundered, and scarcely a family but had seen husband or wife or child laid low by the terrible arrows of these magic clubs. The visitors kept shouting for gold, and when the Indians finally understood and explained that they had none but the little trinkets they wore, the strangers grew fierce. They beat the Indians and shot hundreds of them. Just before sailing back to their homes, the palefaces marched about the villages, seized Indians, and carried them off to the boats. As the strange devil-gods disappeared beyond the horizon, wails rose from the huts and home fires. Fathers mourned their sons, men sorrowed for their wives, children cried for their mothers — all carried off no one knew where in the winged canoes of the terrible white-faces.

Scarcely had the seasons of a year rolled round when again the Indians saw the canoes of the white men returning. This time they were larger and there were more of them. This time the visitors were still more brutal. Even their canoes bellowed and hurled forth fire and smoke. On the great island of Haiti and at a dozen other of the Carib islands, the canoes landed, pouring forth the terrible white men who spread among the frightened Indians like a horrible pestilence.

On and on the white men came. Every season saw more boats pouring forth more of the strange visitors. To every island they came and to the near-by mainland, and finally to every corner of the Indian world.

To the Indians the newcomers were gods or devils. They did not know whence nor why they came. And the men who sailed into the life of the Indians on that fateful twelfth of October, 1492, were equally ignorant about the people and lands that by accident they had discovered.

The strangers came from Europe, a continent where branches of the human race very different from the Indians had been developing customs very different from those that had grown up in America. The various peoples of Europe had been especially successful in inventing implements of all sorts which gave them a great advantage over other people who had not such efficient tools. They used wheels. They used iron. They raised cows and pigs and chickens for food and horses for swift and efficient helpers. They used an alphabet for writing and had invented a printing press which enabled them to make many copies of a single piece of writing and so distribute knowledge widely. They had powder and guns and cannon. They had built huge ships in which they could sail for great distances, using compass and charts to tell where they were and where they were going.

The various nations of western Europe had much in common. They were made up for the most part of somewhat similar

people, members of what is known as the white or Caucasian
race. They had in common their highly developed material
civilization of tools. All of them at just this time were in a
ferment of activity. Populations were increasing and people
needed new worlds in which to settle and carve out careers.
Trade was becoming an increasing source of wealth and
ambition, and individuals and nations were racing to enlarge
their commerce. The Church was seething with activity. The
Spanish had just cast the non-Christian Moors out of Europe
and were eager for new worlds to conquer for their Church.
In other nations, new religious ideas were bursting the bonds
of old dogma and all branches of Christianity were full of
crusading zeal.

From this Europe, with its highly developed tools, its bubbling
energy and ambition, its crusading religion, its lust for trade
and gold, voyagers were setting out to seek fresh countries or
new ways of reaching old ones. Christopher Columbus persuaded Queen Isabella of Spain to equip him with a fleet so
that, by sailing around the world to the westward, he might
find a new passage to Asia and the Indies.

When Columbus surprised the natives of America by landing
on their islands, he thought he had reached the Indies. This
mistake was the more natural since the people he found were
brown-skinned and very like the men of Asia. He naturally
called them 'Indians' and the native Americans have been
known by that name ever since. Columbus never knew, even
until his death ten years later, that he had not found a new route
to India, but had stumbled onto a new world.

To the ambitious people of Europe, it did not much matter
what Columbus had discovered so long as it offered fresh
adventure, the possibility of new wealth, the chance to extend
earthly conquest and heavenly dominion. When Columbus

brought back word of his discovery, all Europe seemed eager to rush to the new world.

Spain as the discoverer was the first to send voyagers into the new land and her conquests were the spectacular events of the century following 1492. With the adventurers came priests, as eager to stake out the claims of the Church as the conquistadores were to enlarge the Spanish domain, as eager to save the souls of the newly found people as the adventurers were to seize their wealth. So was set up from the very beginning that queer partnership between piety and greed which gave so strange a color to much of Europe's conquest of the new world. But the Spaniards came chiefly seeking gold, and in their mad search for wealth and power they overran the islands, stormed the great kingdoms of Middle America, and conquered almost the whole of South America.

The farmers and fishermen of the Carib islands were easily subdued by the invaders. Angered that the islands were not teeming with gold, the Spaniards set about amassing wealth from the abundant man-power. They forced the Indians to labor on farms and mines in order to dig riches for the settlers. Unable to endure this driving labor, the Indians wasted away and died by thousands. Diseases brought in by the white men raged through the native population, killing most of those who escaped slaughter and slavery. As the Indians sickened and died, slaves from Africa were shipped in to work the mines and plantations. Within a generation, the islands, from being wholly Indian, became almost entirely ruled by Spaniards and worked by Negroes.

Soon the Spaniards pushed on to the mainland. The strong Aztec kingdom of Mexico fell. The Maya and the other peoples of Central America were quickly conquered. The great Inca Empire of Peru was crushed. And with the swift loss of the

The Spaniards Led by Cortez

high plateaus of Bolivia and the wide territory now known as Chile, most of the great continent of South America was in the control of the Spanish within half a century of their arrival. Meanwhile, the great eastern section, Brazil, was conquered by Spain's neighbor, Portugal.

While the conquistadores seized power and looted the wealth, priests tried to convert the natives to Christianity and to European ways of living. For the most part, the priests befriended the Indians and tried to protect them from the brutal greed of the adventurers. But to the Indians it was as shameful to lose their faith and independence as it was to give up their land.

After spectacular conquests throughout the sixteenth century, the Spanish momentum began to wear out. But other Europeans followed in even greater numbers as on and on the white men came.

The ships of Champlain sailing up the St. Lawrence and of Hendrik Hudson entering the wide river by Manhattan Island were almost as surprising to the red men of the north as the

Meet the Aztecs

three little sailing vessels of Columbus had been to the natives
of the Carib islands. But the northern Indians did not suffer
as much, for the French and Dutch who followed these explorers did not abuse the natives so greatly. They were interested not in conquest but in trade. The Dutch even traded for
the land they took for their towns, paying, for example, sixty
gulden (the equivalent of twenty-four dollars) for the twenty
thousand acres of woodland that made up the Island of Manhattan. The Dutch had little influence on the Indian world,
for they were quickly supplanted by rival invaders. But the
French were in active contact with the vast interior of North
America for one hundred and fifty years. Missionaries and
explorers as well as traders made trips of hundreds of miles
westward and southward from strong settlements which they
built up and down the St. Lawrence River.

The French did not want to kill the Indians, for they made
their living from the furs which the natives brought in. But
the brandy which the French used as the chief item of barter
destroyed them as effectively as wars, and the diseases which

the traders carried far into the interior weakened and decimated the native population.

Last among the white men to invade the Indians' world were the English. They did not come chiefly for conquest or trade, but to build homes for themselves in the new world. Yet in the end they proved the most destructive of Indian life, for they took the Indians' land for their colonies and, as their settlements grew, they kept pushing the natives back and back.

The English made many attempts before they succeeded in setting up enduring colonies. In 1497 John Cabot sailed an English ship to the islands off the coast of Canada. As early as 1584 settlers came to North Carolina and Virginia. But the Indians drove them off, and it was not until 1607 that the permanent colony of Virginia was established and not until 1620 that the first of the New England settlements was planted by the arrival of the Pilgrims in Plymouth.

The colonists had bitter struggles with the Indians that have been celebrated in chronicles and romances, in poems and sermons, so familiar to every schoolboy that there is no need to repeat them here. The only trouble with the great mass of literature of these heroic days is that it is written from the prejudiced standpoint of the conqueror. An early Pilgrim, for example, thanked God for a pestilence which practically wiped out a whole Massachusetts tribe, saying piously, 'By this means Christ, whose great and glorious works throughout the earth are all for the benefit of his churches and his chosen, not only made room for his people to plant, but also tamed the hearts of the barbarous Indians.' In the fierce partisanship of the early historians, all the staunch defenses and fierce reprisals of the Indians were simply 'dastardly wiles of the savage redskins'; and every defeat and slaughter of the natives a triumph of civilization over barbarism. The fact is that terrible massacres occurred on both sides. Guile and treachery were freely used by both groups. The colonists surged in, sure in their faith in God, arrogant in their race pride, hungry for land for new homes, and by superior force and overwhelming numbers drove the natives out. The Indians, defending their homes and their lives, fought every inch of the way by every weapon of arms and guile they could command.

However long and bitter the struggles, the end was always the same: defeat for the Indians, the loss of more and more land to the white hordes which came pressing onward in ever greater numbers. By 1637, there were twenty thousand British settlers in New England and the whole Atlantic seaboard from Maine to North Carolina was dotted with colonies. In another thirty years, the Indian power in New England was ended and the race almost wiped out from the region. By 1750, the population of the English colonies had grown to one million — probably more than the total native population had ever been throughout the whole area of the present United States — and tens of thousands of white settlers, seeking new lands to farm, were beginning to push westward from the seaboard into the interior.

When the colonies won their independence from England, the new nation began conquering and settling the continent with fresh vigor. In the growing population of the new nation not only English settlers but immigrants from every people of Europe came pouring in — Italians, Poles, Swedes, Germans, Russians, Lithuanians, Czechs, Serbs, Jews.

Before the strong tide of the growing nation, the native population was almost swept away. In the earlier years, much of the energy of the colonists had been spent in wars among themselves and the European nations from which they came. In this strife the several white groups found it profitable to keep

strong Indian tribes about them as allies. But with the unity
and power that came with the independent new nation, there
was no longer need for Indian friendship and there was growing
impatience to clear the land for white settlement.

Americans pushed westward in ever-increasing numbers.
Western New York and the Western Reserve in Ohio were
rapidly filled. Squatters following Daniel Boone poured across
the Appalachian range into Kentucky and Tennessee. With
the purchase of the huge Louisiana Territory and the seizure
of the Southwest from Mexico, Americans swarming into these
freshly opened areas grew more ruthless, more impatient of the
Indians who cumbered their way. When Lewis and Clark
opened the route to the Northwest, and when gold was discovered in California and Colorado, hordes of pioneers set out
in caravans of covered wagons for overland voyages clear to
the Pacific Coast. Soon iron rails and steam engines completed
the conquest of the continent.

The Indians resisted these invasions, but in the end they
were always defeated and forced to move on. Whole tribes
were driven from their original homes back and back, and
finally into the reservations. In the earlier struggles the
Indians fought on something like parity with the colonists:
massacres by white settlers were answered by equally bitter
reprisals from the Indians. But by the early decades of the
nineteenth century, the new nation had grown so powerful
that it moved like a road-roller over the occasional feeble
rebellions of the red men.

As recently as 1890, the last embers of native revolt flamed
and died out. A group of Sioux Indians on their reservation in
South Dakota appeared at the agency complaining of scant
rations and the brutality of the soldiers. The United States
Army moved in, and when the smoke of battle cleared away

the bodies of three hundred Indians were dumped into a common grave.

This was the last stand. The Indians had lost their world. Below the Rio Grande, while the Indian population greatly mixed with foreign elements persists, the patterns of life are largely those introduced from Europe. In the great northern section of the continent, the white man rules supreme, only a few barren reservations being left to the red men. In four brief centuries the old world of the Indian had become the new world of the white man.

A BRONZE RACE
IN A NEW WORLD

THE COMING OF THE WHITE MAN is but a recent episode in the long life of America. The history of the western world starts not in 1492, but in the far distant past when red men — thousands of years before white men dreamed of it — began the peopling of the continent.

Who are these red men? How did it happen that they were living in America? Where did they come from? How did they settle and grow in this part of the world?

No exact answers can be given to these questions. The problems go back into the dim past, long before the time of written history. But there are signs and records of various sorts which make it possible to trace at least the outlines of the origin and growth of the native Americans. Certain of the high Indian civilizations left picture writing carved on stone, fragments of which exist to this day and give us dates and records with which to form a history of more than two thousand years. Other remains in temples and statues, in pottery and metal work, give us pictures of past glories just as the remains of Greek and Latin art give us an insight into the early life of Athens and Rome. Fossils and buried trove of many kinds furnish glimpses into the far distant past. And a comparison of Indians and their ways of life with people of other lands gives us some idea of who the Indians are and how they came here.

There are endless theories and fables about the settling of America. At one time it was thought that ancestors of mankind may have started separately in different parts of the world. By this theory, one race of men grew up in Asia, another in Europe, another in Africa, and still another — the Indians — in America. Another theory is that once a chain of islands stretched across the Pacific Ocean from southern Asia to Peru at the western edge of South America and that yellow men from Asia came across this ancient land bridge which later sank, leaving the adventurers isolated in the new world. As a matter of fact, there is some evidence that a group of islands in the South Pacific may have been submerged by upheavals in the bed of that great ocean. But that was long before human life appeared. If any colonists arrived in the new world by way of the Pacific Ocean, it is probable that they were few in number, coming by canoes long after the continent was fully settled with its original inhabitants.

One legend is that the Indians are the Lost Tribes of Israel whom the Lord punished by sending them to the far continent of America. Stories about the lost continent of Atlantis have also been popular for hundreds of years. Many people have played with the idea that in ancient times Europe and America were one land until suddenly the middle dropped out and Atlantis sank, leaving in its place the ocean which bears its name. Another version of the same myth is that Atlantis, originally a part of Europe, split off and moved westward to form the new continent of America. According to these fables, the Indians are descendants of the people who were living on the western portion of the original continent when Atlantis sank or when it broke off from Europe and gave them a free ride across the Atlantic to the new anchorage.

The myths of various Indian tribes give still other accounts of the origin of the race and the peopling of America: the rising of the red men from a sacred lake or well; the birth of the race from the union of a plumed serpent and a god or from the earth mother and the sun father; the creation of Indians from an earlier race of perfect beings who fell into discord and from whose strife came all living things.

THE SETTLING OF AMERICA

While myths and theories abound, there is now general agreement among all careful students of the subject that Indians are members of that branch of the human family which we call Mongoloid or yellow-brown people; that their ancestors came from Asia to America over a route far to the north where the tips of the two continents almost touch; and that the great double continent of America has been slowly settled during a long period — probably fifteen thousand or twenty thousand years — by the descendants of these early Mongoloid people.

All evidence that we have shows that man did not originate on this continent, but came in from some earlier home. No bones or fossils of really ancient man have ever been found in America such as the relics unearthed in China and Java, South Africa or parts of Europe. And there are no traces here of those early ape-like ancestors of man which have been found near the earliest human bones in the old world. Traces of men so far found in America are thought to go back at most not more

than twenty thousand years — recent times in the slow cycles of human evolution.

The common belief today is that the human race originated somewhere in the great continent of Asia and from there slowly spread outward in many directions. In course of time, individual groups of mankind, branching off from the original stock and living for thousands of years in their separate parts of the world, formed strains of such differences as to produce what we call today the various races of man. The largest of these divisions we roughly classify as white, black, and yellow-brown.

While the blacks grew up largely in Africa and the whites in western Asia and Europe, the third great branch of the human race — the yellow-brown or Mongoloid people — filled eastern Asia and many of the islands to the south and east. It is thought that, as the land became crowded and the population continued to multiply, these yellow people moved farther and farther out from their original source, pushing, on the one hand, to south Asia and the Pacific Ocean and, on the other hand, into northeast Asia, until they occupied all the land up to the northern and eastern tip of Siberia. Then, perhaps because game and fish got scarce or some warring tribe attacked them from behind, a few of these early Mongoloid people at the eastern edge of Siberia looked across the narrow strait to the fresh and unoccupied land of North America and moved over to it.

Certainly the simplest and easiest way into America from the old world is by this northern route across the narrow strip of water known as Bering Strait. On a clear day it is possible to stand at the northeast tip of Siberia and, looking across about thirty-five miles of ocean, see the headlands of Alaska and the northwest tip of America. It is probable that in earlier times the channel was even narrower than now because of the presence of islands — stepping-stones from Asia to America — which have since been covered by the sea. At any rate, there is a very small space between the continents at this northern point, a gap which even primitive people, by the use of crude rafts or by trekking across the ice in winter, could easily cross.

At first probably only a few families came over to this new land. But as pressure continued in Asia others followed year after year, century after century. Once on the new continent it was natural for the settlers to spread out and move onto unoccupied land, especially to the milder climates of the south. In the course of hundreds of years — maybe thousands of years — this natural movement spread the settlers over the whole of the great double continent of America.

There are many proofs that Indians are of a single stock — Mongoloid. They all have yellowish-brown skin. Their hair is black and coarse and straight and they have little hair on their bodies or faces. They have dark eyes, set far apart, and high cheek bones. Their noses, like other Mongolians', are often long and beaked and in width are about midway between the thin noses of whites and the thick broad noses of Africans.

Even with a similar ancestry and a continuous life within a single continent, there are great differences among the various Indian tribes. It is probable that the people kept trickling over from Asia during long periods of time. There may have been hundreds of years between the coming of one group and another, and these several groups may have been made up of slightly different kinds of Mongoloid people who from era to era occupied the eastern tip of Siberia. Furthermore, as the immigrants arrived in Alaska, they moved on down by various routes into the warmer and more hospitable climates. One group moved to the great plains section of what is now the United States, others eastward to the waters and rolling hills of the St. Lawrence Valley or on to those warmer regions along the southern Atlantic coast which we now call the Carolinas, Georgia, Florida. Great numbers settled in the very warm climate of Mexico and Central America. And still others pushed on across the narrow isthmus which connects the two halves of the continent and started the dense populations of South America. The groups living in given territories naturally resented and opposed the coming of others. Therefore later streams of people had to search out fresh areas until all of the habitable parts of North and South America were filled.

Having settled in various parts of this great continent, groups lived together for hundreds or thousands of years, cut off almost completely from people of other customs. Each group built its life on the basis of the habits it had brought with it and on the environment of its new home. Thus various tribes or peoples developed ways of life distinct unto themselves, with their own language, their own arts and tools, their own religion and customs.

Where farming was well developed, the people multiplied; where living came chiefly from hunting and fishing and foraging, the numbers were very small, even over wide areas. It is probable that in all North America above Mexico there were never more than a million Indians; in Mexico and Central America, with highly developed agricultural civilizations, probably three million; in South America, with intensive farming and a carefully planned economy, possibly four or five million, chiefly concentrated about the fertile plateaus of Peru and Ecuador. In all there were probably not more than ten million Indians in native America.

A SEPARATE LIFE IN AMERICA

Because of the long isolation of the whole American continent, the tools and crops and ways of life which developed here were strikingly different from those found in other parts of the world. Two streams of human development grew up at the same time: one all by itself in the new world; the other constantly enriched by exchange of ideas and practices between various peoples who were in contact with one another throughout the several parts of the old world.

Human progress comes most effectively from the exchange of inventions and practices and ideas among different groups of people. It was natural that civilization should flourish in the Near East and Mediterranean basin for there a great many active peoples were in close touch with one another. For example, the early agriculture of Egypt was passed on — slowly, it is true, but steadily — to surrounding people. The art and philosophy of Greece were scattered like refreshing rain to 'savages' who might never on their own initiative have developed such things. When one people in the old world invented such elementary tools as the wheel or the use of iron, those marvelous devices were passed on to other less ingenious folk who at once benefited by them and who in turn might develop them to further uses which again would be passed back to the original inventors.

The Indians in America, isolated from the rest of the world, did not have the benefit of the inventions and suggestions of other people. During all that period when Egypt and Greece and Mesopotamia were actively developing their arts and sciences around the borders of the Mediterranean Sea, when the Arabs were contributing their mathematical science and Rome was perfecting a system of law and government and spreading knowledge throughout a large part of the western world, when even the contributions of Asia were in some slight exchange with Europe — during all this time the Indians were isolated in remote America; they had to make all their inventions for themselves and work out all their practices without the aid of the experience of other people.

While civilization in America suffered greatly from this lack of contact with other active peoples, there was some exchange of ideas and inventions among the several tribes. The cultivation of maize and other crops, when perfected by one group, spread slowly to others. Similarly, the arts and the social and religious customs which grew up among one tribe influenced the practices of its neighbors. Contact among the various Indian peoples was greatest where the two continents meet in Middle America and here the highest civilizations grew up. But in general in America there was much less enriching exchange than that which took place among the peoples of the old world.

THE GROWTH OF INDIAN CULTURE

The red men came into America when the human race was in a very primitive stage of development, an era which we now refer to as the stone age. When these people broke their contact with Asia they were wandering bands of nomads or hunters, knowing nothing about even the crudest farming and lacking many of the most elementary tools. Probably about all that the ancestors of the Indians brought with them from Asia were the ability to make fire by drilling one stick of wood into another; the dog as a domesticated animal; stone implements for cutting and scraping; the spear, spear thrower, and harpoon, together with some crude ideas of weaving nets and baskets. They also brought with them special traditions of social organization and religious observances.

The Indians developed certain tools and usages far beyond the primitive store brought over by their stone-age ancestors. But many things which were later perfected in Europe or Asia never came into being in native America. All the great wealth of domesticated animals, for example, that transformed life elsewhere, was never known to Indians. Cattle, sheep, goats, pigs, horses, which seem to us such primary necessities of any comfortable life, were entirely absent from America until the white man brought them in. Many of the staple crops were also lacking: wheat, barley, rice. The plow was unknown so that, having neither plow nor draft animal, the Indian had to cultivate his farm crudely and ineffectively by hand or with sharpened sticks. Stringed instruments were not developed and the Indians were restricted in their music to drums and flutes and rattles. The alphabet was not known and, although certain advanced groups used picture writing and a very efficient number system, no rich and full literature has come down to us to commemorate the arts and achievements of the ancient

Indian civilizations in the way that the writings of classic poets and historians immortalize the glory that was Greece and the grandeur that was Rome. Iron was unknown — a metal so important to material progress that its discovery and use elsewhere brought in a radically new era in human affairs known throughout history as the iron age.

Most amazing of all, the Indian never invented the wheel. A whole great series of civilizations grew up covering half the world for thousands of years without hitting upon this which is one of the most elemental and useful of all human devices. Even in the making of pottery, one of the most universal of Indian arts, there was no potter's wheel. There were no carts or pulleys. No water wheel ever helped in the grinding of corn; no windmill pumped water from the deep wells. No wheel ever turned throughout the whole wide expanse of this great continent from the beginning of time until the introduction of European tools a few brief centuries ago.

Isolation, while it meant lack of many useful inventions of other parts of the world, saved the native Americans from certain of the old world ills. Many of the great contagious diseases which afflicted mankind in Europe and Africa and Asia were happily absent from America. The Indians, of course, had their own diseases: fevers, eye sores, intestinal disturbances, rheumatism. But they were free from the greater plagues. Unfortunately, they have had to pay for that earlier freedom by a lack of immunity to the old world ills and hence great suffering when these diseases arrived. The terrible scourges of tuberculosis and smallpox were unknown during the thousands of years of Indian history. But when the white man brought these diseases, smallpox mowed down the red men more devastatingly than European bullets and tuberculosis continues to destroy Indians who have withstood all other attacks. Even measles, which with the white man was a mild disease chiefly of children, found the Indian helplessly susceptible and flamed up into death-dealing epidemics. Yellow fever, which during recent centuries raged throughout tropical America, was absent until brought over in slave ships from Africa. Hookworm infection, which has spread over all the warmer parts of the new world, was unknown in ancient America. Although the Indians had many eye troubles, they did not suffer from the blinding disease of trachoma.

PRODUCTS OF THE INDIAN WORLD

While the Indian never happened upon many of the inventions which we regard as basic, and while he differed from the old world in his customs and practices, he had not stood still since his ancestors first came to the new world.

In agriculture he produced an ample and nourishing subsistence. Because of the different plants found in a wild state in the old world and the new, the crops grown by the Indian are very different from those which had been developed on other continents. The greatest of the native American staples is maize, or Indian corn. This crop was the basis of Indian agriculture. It was to America what rice has been to Asia. Beans and squashes were also raised by Indians throughout many parts of the Americas. In the warmer regions, especially amid the high civilizations of Mexico and Central America and Peru, many other important plants were cultivated: potatoes, sweet potatoes, chili peppers, tomatoes, tobacco, and the cocoa bean for the making of chocolate. Cotton and sisal were widely grown and woven into cloth.

As contrasted to the rich variety of native crops, the Indian did not have many animals which could be domesticated and had to build his civilization without them. The dog followed him from Asia and has been a part of Indian life for all time, used not only for companionship and protection but in many places for meat, and among the Eskimo and the buffalo-hunting tribes of the Great Plains as a draft animal for drawing sledges and tent poles. Bees were cultivated by many of the more settled tribes, honey being the only sweet generally known in native America, though certain tribes of the Northeast took maple sugar from the trees and the Peruvians made a kind of syrup from green corn stalks. The only other animals tamed for use were the llamas, small wool-bearing camels grown in Peru, and turkeys, which were domesticated in the Middle American regions and among the Pueblo Indians.

The native Americans made but a few basic inventions in tools and science but they carried these to great heights. We are amazed that a people should have advanced as far as certain Indian tribes did without discovering iron which is so useful in the making of efficient tools. Yet they used other metals with the greatest skill and the highest art. Gold and silver, copper and tin were wrought and smelted into objects which rank among the world's finest jewels. Platinum and gold were blended by a process unknown to the modern world until recent analysis of ancient Peruvian ornaments revealed it. In the absence of cutting instruments of iron and steel, the Middle American artists sharpened stones and split off flakes of obsidian and so made knives and chisels with which they carved some of the most beautiful and graceful sculpture of world history. The skilful and varied use of stone and wood for weapons and tools and building materials is an example of the high and wide development to which Indians carried a single basic process.

Pottery and basket making the Indians also carried to a high point of art as well as utility. These crafts were so widespread among the tribes of both North and South America that the making of pots and baskets became almost universal Indian arts. The greatest variety of fibers and patterns were used in baskets. Vases and urns were fashioned by many ingenious methods and through the use of almost every possible material. Spinning and weaving were also developed widely, although thread was usually just twisted between thumb and finger and only hand looms were used for weaving. In certain regions, especially Peru, textiles were among the highest of the fine arts.

Boats were made by many tribes which lived near the water. In regions where there were large trees, canoes were made by hollowing out great logs. Elsewhere light wooden frames were covered with bark or skins, the finest examples being the birch-bark canoes of the eastern woodlands and Great Lakes and the sealskin kayaks of the Eskimo.

In building their homes the Indians used many different materials and designs: the stone and plaster pueblos of the Southwest; the cedar houses of the far Northwest with skilful carpentry and elaborate carvings; the earth-covered, log hogans of the Navajos; the skin tipis of the Plains Indians; the bark and pole houses of the Iroquois. Among the highly developed peoples of Middle America and Peru, building went much further. Stone was used to build spacious and beautiful temples and palaces richly ornamented with carvings.

The greatest intellectual contributions of the Indians were in mathematics and astronomy. The Maya devised a place system of numbers with a zero long before the decimal system was used in Europe. The Middle American people also developed astronomy to an elaborate science. Recording with their flexible number system and observing with exactness over long periods of time, they were able to construct a calendar of amazing accuracy and to predict movements of the heavenly bodies, including eclipses, with a precision unapproached by the highest scholars of the time in Europe and Asia.

In contrast to the small number of tools and material inventions, the various Indian groups developed a rich and complex social and cultural life. So great was the variation in the customs of the many tribes that it is impossible to make general statements to cover all of them. A true picture can be given only by examples.

The high Indian cultures grew up at the crossroads of the double continent: in Central America, Mexico, and Peru

CLASSIC INDIAN CULTURES

IN AMERICA, AS IN THE OLD WORLD, certain peoples created arts and learning far beyond their neighbors. Just as Greece produced a culture finer than that of other nations of early Europe, so in the new world the Maya developed fine arts and science to such a point that they have come to be regarded as creators of the classic civilization of the Indians. And just as Rome developed aspects of civilization that placed it also among the European classics, so the Aztec and Inca are properly included among the classic cultures of America.

The early centers of art and learning grew up in the areas around the narrow neck of land where the two halves of the American continent meet. People moving back and forth between North and South America came into contact at this bottle neck of Middle America. This area naturally became a place of exchange of arts and inventions among the various tribes and a place where diverse people intermarried, thus setting up a cross fertilization of both blood and ideas. It was natural, therefore, that the high classic cultures of native America should grow up at this crossroads of the double continent: in Central America, Mexico, and Peru.

THE MAYA

THREE OR FOUR THOUSAND YEARS AGO, a special group of Indians made their home in that narrow neck of land between the two American continents which now is Guatemala, Honduras, and Yucatan. They were made up of a number of tribes, but most of them spoke the same language, with varying dialects, and the whole group were nearly enough alike to be regarded as one people, the Maya.

In the fertile region of Central America these people began to change from a roving life of hunting and fishing to a more settled life in villages. The change was made possible by the great discovery that maize or Indian corn could be planted and harvested. This idea, which seems to us today so simple as to be a matter of course, meant a veritable transformation of life to the ancients.

Until planting and harvesting were invented there was no settled life. There was only a nomadic existence — wandering about, hunting, fishing, living on wild herbs and roots. In all parts of the world the discovery of agriculture was the beginning of human advancement. Egypt developed one of the earliest civilizations because in the fertile valley of the Nile her people were among the first to take up farming. So in the new world the people who began to farm began also to build up the arts and crafts and social forms that go with settled life.

Agriculture in America grew up about maize. There is in Middle America a wild grass that is very much like maize, well named by certain of the Indian tribes *teocentli*, 'grass of the gods.' Probably a variety of this grass was turned into true maize, producing the rich yellow ears of corn on which men in America have thrived ever since. Then, in the course of time it was found that it was not necessary to wait for this wild grain to grow wherever it happened to, but that seeds could be planted in convenient fields and that from such planting a much more abundant harvest could be counted upon regularly year after year.

Even with the great discovery of planting and harvesting, the Maya did not carry on farming in a way that we would regard as efficient. They had no draft animals and no iron tools. The cultivation of their farms was elemental. First they cleared the land of the forests and underbrush which grew luxuriously in this fertile country. Since they could not chop down the big trees with their crude stone knives and axes, they simply cut as deeply as they could through the bark all around the tree and left it to die. The smaller brush they tore up by the roots or trampled down. This killing of the forest they did at the end of the rainy season which lasts regularly about half of every year. Then, having left the trees and brush to die and dry up during the five or six rainless months, they set fire to the dry timber and burned over the whole field.

In this rudely prepared farm they then planted the corn by equally primitive methods. An Indian with a sharp stick in one hand and a bag of corn in the other would stride over the field. At every second step he would drive the stick into the ground and drop a few kernels into the hole made by the stick, scraping the earth over the seed with his bare foot as he strode on. In time it was found that beans and squash could be planted and harvested as well as maize. So, often a friendly bean or two was dropped in with the corn. And squashes were dribbled along in the corn field or on separate patches of land.

Later other food plants were discovered, some of them known only to the new world and all of them important crops in America to this day: tomatoes, chili peppers, sweet potatoes, cocoa. In addition, fibrous plants were grown, one of which — cotton — has come to be among the most notable of modern American crops. A strange weed was found that was pleasant to smoke and that gave off a pungent fragrance when used as incense in the temples, and from that weed has grown one of America's greatest products — tobacco.

By cruel experience the early farmers found that the second year after it had been cleared a field would produce only about three fourths as much corn as it did at first, and the third year less than half as much. So the Indians formed the practice of clearing new land every year or two and letting the old field grow back into brush and forest. After a regrowth of five or ten years the abandoned field would be cut and burned over and again used for planting. This was laborious farming. It was also wasteful of land. In course of time the forests ceased to grow; the farm land began to wear out. But it was the only way these people knew to raise their crops. And there was enough forest land for them to go on for hundreds of years, moving from field to field with their simple planting.

El Caracol, Astronomical Observatory, Chichen Itza, Yucatan

ART AND LEARNING

With settled homes and with food coming in regularly and plentifully, the Maya began to give to arts and learning a part of that energy which heretofore had been put into wresting a living from wild nature. It was natural that this people, depending for their new way of life upon agriculture, should have begun to study the seasons which regulated the cycle of planting and harvesting. And it was natural, too, that they should carry their interest back to the movements of the sun and moon and stars which marked the changing seasons. The unusual thing was that the Maya made these studies so carefully and wisely that they brought astronomy to a point far beyond anything known at the time anywhere else in the world. They watched the changing positions of the sun, the moon, and the planets from day to day, month to month, year to year. They began to make up a calendar. After countless observations and records, they not only listed the relative positions of the heavenly bodies over a long period of the past but also began to foretell the positions

Face signs for numbers 1 and 5
On temples and monuments the Maya used a system of individual
numbers from one to twenty

of the stars in the future, including eclipses of the sun and moon
and the changing positions of that morning and evening star
which we call Venus.

Along with astronomy, the Maya developed a system of
numbers, as big a jump in the realm of abstract ideas as the
planting of maize had been in practical affairs. They invented
a series of numbers with a place system, using the very abstract concept of zero as a means of indicating place. This is
what we use in the decimal system. The Maya, however,
counted by multiples of twenty, while we use multiples of ten.
The high intelligence required for this invention of a place system
with a zero is clear when we remember that the best Europe
invented were the crude Roman numerals. All the science of
the old world civilizations had to stumble along with these un-
wieldy symbols until the Arabs (refining a concept of ancient
India) invented the decimal system a thousand years or more
after the Maya had perfected their highly efficient arithmetic.

People engaged in building up a civilization also need a
system of writing. The Maya did not make as brilliant progress
here as they did in numbers. They did not invent an alphabet.
They simply reduced picture writing to an abbreviated form —
using parts of a picture to stand for an entire object or even for
an idea: a beak for a bird, tears for rain, pictures of war captives

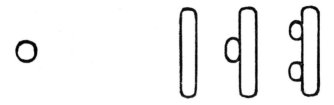

Numerals 1, 5, 6, and 7
*The Maya also used this number system which was very much
like Roman numerals*

to show a military victory. They may have worked out the
beginnings of phonetic writing, but modern study of the few
surviving examples of Maya picturegraphs has made little
headway in reading anything but the calendar signs. Except
for their very accurate system of recording dates, the Maya
picturegraphs seem a less efficient system of writing than the
hieroglyphs of the ancient Egyptians.

Another way in which high cultures find expression is in art.
In this realm, especially in sculpture and architecture, the
Maya attained distinction comparable to the finest classics of
the old world. Most of the remains that have come down
to us from the Maya civilization are in the form of art: magnificent temples, often standing on pyramids built to serve as
platforms; beautiful statues; a veritable riot of carvings. Even
the computations of the calendar appear in elaborate carvings on stone pillars or in intricate picturegraphs as notable
for their artistry as for their learning.

RELIGION

Art and science were but the handmaidens of religion, which
was the great force in Maya life. All human and material affairs
were thought of as depending on the pleasure or anger of the
gods. The rains came and went at divine will. Health and

Temple of Two Lintels at Chichen Itza

disease, prosperity and poverty, even life and death were gifts or punishments. To ward off evil and to win favor with the gods were the most important things in life.

Farming is notably dependent upon the whims of nature: rains, drought, insects, the fertility of seeds and land. The primitive Maya farmers, little versed in scientific agriculture, attributed the success or failure of their crops to direct acts of those gods who controlled the rain and wind or who were in special charge of maize or beans or cotton. It was necessary to plant and reap on just those days that were most pleasing to the gods who ruled over the particular seasons and the given crops.

Since the seasons were evidently controlled by the movements of the earth and the heavenly bodies, the study of astronomy — which the Maya carried to so high a point — was a religious study, an attempt to find out the devious ways in which the gods worked. The calendar was a record of the wonders they performed and an attempt to find ways of fitting the acts of man to the divine will.

Naturally a great priesthood grew up to mediate between men and gods. These priests had enormous power since they were thought to be in touch with the divine beings and thus able to protect men from their anger and to find ways of bringing good luck in crops, in health, in marriage, in battle, in every conceivable aspect of life. Learning was entirely in the hands of the priests. The picture writing and the symbols used in the calendars and on the carvings and decorations of the buildings were sealed books to the common people. Only delegates of the gods were allowed to have anything to do with such matters, and a large part of the training of novices was not only in religious lore but in the sciences of mathematics and astronomy and the arts of writing and sculpture. The priests thus were not only in charge of the morals and daily lives of the people; they were also the force which advanced learning and promoted the arts.

The Maya had as many gods and goddesses as the Greeks and Romans, and these gods — like those of classic Europe — were full of curious human qualities and weaknesses. As might be expected among a people whose whole existence depended upon the harvests, the most important of their deities had to do with agriculture and fertility. Gods of the rain and the wind, gods of thunder and lightning, gods of the several seasons, even of all the various days of the calendar, are found in statues and carvings up and down the land.

The king of the Maya gods was Itzamna — corresponding to the Zeus of Greece or Jupiter of Rome. Itzamna was the personification of the east and the rising sun, of light, life, and knowledge. He was thought of as the founder of Maya civilization, the first priest of Maya religion, the inventor of writing and books, the great healer.

The god best known to us, however, is Kukulcan, the feathered serpent. His image is found on temples and statues throughout Mayaland and far into other lands which were

Restoration of the Temple of Kukulcan at Chichen Itza

influenced by the Maya and their neighbors: Mexico, Central America, and even the Pueblo country of the American Southwest. The feathered serpent often serves in late Maya architecture as the column did in Greece. The serpent god's head — with its plume of feathers and its open jaws often holding a human face — rests on the ground to form the pedestal, while his serpent tail stretches upward to form the shaft of the pillar. In legend Kukulcan was originally a ruler of the neighboring Toltec people. And he is given so many of the qualities of a human leader that it is likely he was an actual hero of early history whose life and deeds were glorified in song and story until in course of time he came to be regarded as a god. In Maya mythology he is the great organizer, the builder of cities, the framer of laws, the teacher of the calendar.

The deity most feared and hated was Ahpuch, the god of death. He is pictured as a fleshless skull. 'Old barebones,' one chronicle calls him. He was subjected to caricature in art and to curses and revilings in ceremonies and in daily life. Ahpuch was the chief of a series of gods who impersonated evil and bad luck, who stood as a kind of opposing army to the gods of life and fertility and learning. Thus religion with the Maya, as with many people, was a fairly balanced struggle between the powers of good and evil, of light and darkness.

Goddesses held a minor place. Ixchel, the rainbow, was thought of as the bride of Itzamna and as the goddess of child-birth and medicine. Other goddesses were patrons of hunting, of painting, and of jade carving. But in general the divine women were of small consequence compared to the powerful and picturesque male gods.

The Maya believed in immortality, but not in a physical life after death. The spirit was thought of as enjoying a heaven or a hell on the basis of the individual's actions during life and the manner of his death. Heaven was guaranteed to all persons who died in battle, who were offered as living sacrifices, and — odd as it seems to us — who killed themselves. Thus war, human sacrifice, and suicide became holy acts.

Sacrifice played a large part in the religious rites. In the first flowering of the Maya culture there was little human sacrifice, though there was a great deal of purification by blood through the slaughtering of animals, especially birds, on the sacred altars, and also by the piercing of the tongue or other tender flesh of human penitents and allowing the blood to flow over the images of the gods. With the Maya, as with almost all Indian tribes, great stress was placed on purification before any religious rite. Novitiates or priests who were to endure some trial or lead some ceremony were required to fast for hours, often for days. Then, just before they started the rite, they were given a powerful emetic so that they would disgorge any food remaining in their stomachs. They were also given long sweat baths to purge their bodies of impurities. Only when clean of body and open of mind was the novitiate or priest supposed to present himself before the gods.

During the second era of Maya greatness, when religion had grown more formal and more cruel, human sacrifice became a regular and frequent part of worship. Prisoners of war were

Maya priest

slaughtered, often in great numbers, and their bleeding hearts
torn from their bodies and flung upon the images of the gods.
Citizens also were sacrificed, being chosen by lot or by magic
for this rôle which was a highly prized honor. Young girls,
selected for their beauty and nobility, were reared in nunneries,
kept pure and taught modesty and graceful manners in order
that they might serve the deities. And those who distinguished
themselves in purity and grace were awarded the highest of

Maya honors. They became brides of the gods through being hurled into the sacred wells or by having their hearts torn out and offered upon the altars of the temples. Many romantic tales have been woven by modern writers about the supposed terrors of these victims, especially about the thwarted love affairs of the sacred virgins. But it was probably all taken as a matter of course.

LIFE AMONG THE MAYA

For the common people life flowed along in regular orderly channels. The round of planting and harvesting, the tasks of spinning, weaving, and pottery making, were interspersed with rites and ceremonies in the cities. The festivals became market days as well. As men, women, and children trudged in for a ceremony, the fields about the city teemed with temporary thatch shelters and with booths for the barter of all kinds of foods and products. Corn cakes, beans, squash, and small rabbitlike animals caught in the bush were offered to delight the appetite and were traded for gourds, pottery, fiber mats, hides, and cotton fabrics. Ornaments were also on sale: beautiful feather shawls, beads, pendants of jade, and bells of gold.

As the time approached for a temple ceremony, people would pour into the broad plazas and swarm over the steps of near-by buildings, patiently squatting on their haunches if they arrived ahead of time, and standing, eagerly watching as offerings were made to the gods or as ceremonial dances were performed and sacred incantations made.

The people who gathered at such a festival would show some striking features. Their foreheads would slant back sharply from their eyebrows. A peaked head was considered so essential to good looks among the Maya that boards were bound to babies' heads to produce this slanting forehead, much as the feet

Maya market

of girls were deformed by binding in order to make them beautiful in old China. Crossed eyes were also very fashionable. Mothers would tie bits of wood or strings of beads so that they would hang dangling between babies' eyes in order that they would turn inward and so become fixed in this stylish mode. Teeth were filed to points and sometimes studded with bits of jade. The faces of the men and the breasts of the women were often tattooed in elaborate patterns.

Men customarily wore a breechcloth, often carefully embroidered and decorated with feathers. No other garment adorned the average man, though many of them might have sandals made of hemp or skin and here and there a dudish fellow might have a square cape thrown over his shoulders or a carved stone pendant hanging around his neck. Men of high rank wore much more elaborate clothing. Wooden helmets sat awkwardly but fashionably upon their heads, and from these hats hung streamers made of cloth or woven from the gay plumage of the many birds that filled the forests. Rich mantles of jaguar skin were wrapped about the shoulders of the priests and nobles, and finely wrought circles of gold and jade adorned their necks and chests and arms.

Women usually wore a single loose garment, called *huipil*. Gathered about the neck and with slits for the arms, this dress hung like a sack from the shoulders to the feet. Sometimes they wore simply a skirt, leaving the upper body bare save for the tattoo drawings on the skin.

Chastity was a virtue highly regarded and very generally followed by Maya women who were modest and even shy in their relations with men. Meeting a man on the road they would step aside, turning their backs and hiding their faces. Maya women bathed often, going to great pains to keep water at hand in stone vats and earthen jars, and were devoted to flowers and perfumes. It was recorded that the lady of quality 'daily massages her body with a pottery brick impregnated with sweet-smelling gum.'

Young people married at about the age of twenty. The young husband moved into the house of his bride's parents and was compelled to work five years for them before he could set up a house for himself. Widows and widowers remarried as a matter of course. It is recorded that any widow who got a widower to eat a meal in her house had by that act married him. A man or woman obtained a divorce simply by walking out of the house. While divorce — or desertion — was common, it was frowned upon. Polygamy was unknown.

Life was largely communal or co-operative. At times of planting and harvesting, bands of twenty or more would pass from farm to farm and quickly finish the work. Similarly, bands of fifty would join together to hunt deer or pig or the dangerous but beautifully pelted jaguar. While there was private property in homes and crops and craft products, the land was thought of as belonging to the whole people. Many public facilities were also held in common, such as the huge granaries in which corn was stored against possible bad seasons and famines.

Slavery existed in very much the form known in ancient Greece. War captives made up most of the slaves, though citizens might be enslaved for debts or misdeeds. It meant no special disgrace. Slaves could work out their freedom, and servitude was not passed down as a permanent condition from parents to children.

Hospitality throughout Mayaland was full and free; any stranger was taken in and fed even to the last crumb in the house. This was the invariable law with the common people. But with the nobles entertainment was a ritual. Expensive feasts were common in the cities. Often a chief would give a banquet to forty or fifty of his peers, with hired entertainment in the form of music and dancing and with gifts and exquisite vases or cloaks woven from bright feathers as favors for each of the guests. The food included roast meats, vegetable stews, corn cakes, and steaming bowls of chocolate. At the end of the repast beautiful girls served as cup-bearers and so vigorously plied the men with wine that they all got drunk; and as the night wore on wives had to come to drag their besotted husbands home. These feasts had to be returned by every man who attended. This was a debt of honor. Not even death could wipe out the obligation, and orphans received as part of their legacy any unpaid credits or debits of their fathers in the exchange of entertainment.

A favorite pastime was telling stories. History, myths, and dramatic poems were recited over and over to eager listeners. A classic saga was the story of creation. The gods, according to this legend, were not satisfied with an earth which did not have creatures who could praise and worship them. So they decided to make man. They tried three times before they got what they wanted. First they made men of mud, but they were too soft and melted away. Then they carved creatures out of wood. But they did not suit either. The animals and the tools rose up in rebellion against these wooden men. The dogs said, 'You beat us with sticks and order us about; why should we not kill you?' The stones used in grinding corn said, 'In your service we are worn away; day after day you are always rubbing us together, making us go holi, holi, huki, huki; now we will try our strength against you.' In the end, the gods sent a great flood, wiping out these unsatisfactory creatures, and finally fashioned four new men out of corn meal with corn cobs for arms and legs. 'These men were our forefathers,' the saga says, 'four in number were the men created from maize, and afterward four women were made for these men.' Then at last the sun rose, for up to that time the world had been in darkness. And the morning and the evening were the first day, and man, ruling the earth and praising the gods, was started on his way.

Such stories were told over and over among the Maya until they became set in a formal rhythmic style, just as the Homeric poems are supposed to have been recited and polished generation after generation among the ancient Greeks, or as the early Hebrews chanted psalms and tales of prehistoric times long before they wrote them into the books we know as the Old Testament of the Bible. After the Spaniards introduced an alphabet, the old Maya stories were written into books, known as the Chilan Balam and the Popol Vuh, and from these pithy chronicles we get much of our knowledge of Maya life. Some of these stories are still told among the descendants of the Maya, more than a million of whom live today in Yucatan and Central America in a world that has but faint resemblance to the ancient greatness.

MAYA HISTORY

From the scant records that have come down to us, it is evident that there were two great periods in Maya culture. The first started at about the beginning of our calendar, that is, at about the time of the birth of Christ, and reached its height during the centuries from about 600 to 800 A.D. This culture, growing from slow developments which had been going on for one or two thousand years, flowered in Central America in the area which is now Guatemala and Honduras. It grew up around city-states, somewhat like the city-states of ancient Greece. These towns were public and religious centers rather than cities in our sense of the word. The masses of the people lived in little farm hamlets scattered over the near-by area. The capital cities

Maya farm house

were centers of government, religion, and scholarship, rallying points for large populations that lived within a radius of fifteen miles or more from the temple plazas.

Of these cities, Copan in southern Central America was the most highly developed in both art and science. Her buildings were graceful and beautiful, her sculpture the finest in classic America, and her picture writing and calendar stones show an extent and depth of learning exceeding that of other Maya cities. Near Copan is a huge monument made of a single block of stone thirty-five feet long and weighing more than fifty tons. Admiration and wonder are aroused at the mere labor of quarrying this great slab of rock, moving it to the place where it was set up, and completely covering its sides with intricate carvings — all without draft animals, wheeled vehicles of any sort, or metal tools. On a hillside at the edge of the city are the ruins of an ancient sun dial more than four miles across with great pillars at either side. The days when the sun set in direct line with these pillars were the beginning and the end of the Maya

Example of Maya pottery from Guatemala

agricultural year, days which in our calendar are April 9 and September 2.

Many other cities throughout the region have left evidences of their art and learning. Tikal, Palenque, and Quirigua are especially well known for the remains of their beautiful temples, gracefully carved pillars, exquisite pottery, jade ornaments, and intricately inscribed stones.

Just as all these city centers were at the height of their achievement, the early Maya civilization dissolved and disappeared. It is one of the unexplained dramas of history. Agriculture seemed to be advancing with new food and fiber plants being discovered and added to the older staples, thus steadily raising the standard of living. The population seemed to be flourishing and increasing, for there was a constant building of new temple cities. The scholars were busy observing and recording the movements of the heavenly bodies and extending their calendar charts ever further both into the future and into the past. Beautiful temples were being built all over the realm to the increasing glory of the gods, while the carvings and picture writings were establishing an everlasting place in art for the creators. Then swiftly nothing.

Example of Maya pottery from Yucatan

Many guesses have been made as to the cause of the decline: conquest by neighboring tribes, epidemics of disease, some sudden shift in climate. But there is no evidence to support any of these theories. The most likely cause is that the farm lands — burned over and over in the Maya's crude methods of cultivation — ceased to yield crops. Swelling populations and decreasing fertility of the land may have met in a threat of starvation that drove the people to hunt new fields. Or it may be, as some historians claim, that civilizations run in a regular cycle of life like individual human beings — rising with youthful vigor to a plateau of mature competence and then dropping off again to weakness and senility. By such a theory the early Maya culture may have burned so brilliantly that it brought a swift decline, just as the intensive cultivation of the fields brought them to a sterile state.

The dates on the monuments stop abruptly at about the year 800 A.D. While Copan and certain neighboring towns were deserted earlier, the great majority of cities seem to have been in full flower right to the end of the period. Within a few generations the whole group of the early Maya cities were abandoned or had ceased to produce the art and science which had made them notable.

Then followed an interval of two or three hundred years when the Maya were moving the centers of their art and organization north into the peninsula of Yucatan — a period that might be called the Maya Dark Ages. The people were carving out fresh home lands on a new frontier. Their whole energies were given to prospecting and pioneering. It took time to build up farming, to establish homes, and to get a stable enough means of livelihood to have leisure and surplus energy for art and study. Several centuries were spent by the Maya in establishing their roots in the new soil.

The first city to appear in the new empire is Chichen Itza, which means 'beside the wells of the Itza.' This name introduces a new tribe of the Maya people, the Itza, a vigorous stock which dominated the renaissance. It also showed the new importance of water. On the flat and barren plain of Yucatan there are practically no streams, and water is supplied almost wholly by natural wells or underground springs, called *cenotes*. These wells played a large part in the second stage of Maya history; they determined the location of the cities; they took on a sacred character because of their vital importance to life. Certain of them, notably the one at Chichen Itza, became the scene of a spectacular form of human sacrifice: the casting of victims or the plunging of zealous volunteers into the deep and holy waters.

The new centers started slowly and falteringly. Even the early settlement at Chichen Itza was abandoned for a time, and one of the early chronicles remarks, 'Those of the Itza were under the trees, under the boughs, under the branches, to their sorrow.' In time they resettled Chichen Itza and built it into a magnificent sacred city.

With the rebuilding of Chichen Itza in about 1000 A.D., the second great period of Maya culture began. Cities sprang up throughout the new realm of Yucatan with a zest and magnificence comparable to the earlier era. Although the Itza furnished much of the early leadership, the renaissance was more than the expression of a single tribe. Maya-speaking peoples came pouring in from Chiapas and Tabasco to mix with the streams that had come from the south. Influences began to come down also from the north, from the central plateau of Mexico where a new people, the Toltecs, were rising with fresh vigor. With farms established and livelihood provided in abundance, all these diverse but related peoples began to pour their surplus energies again into art and learning. The renaissance saw buildings of size and beauty even beyond those of the first empire. But the sculpture and the scholarship never again equalled the early days. The art and science were more a copying and enlarging of the classic period than the creation of anything new and distinctive. The religion also took on greater formality and cruelty. It was a magnificent reflowering but it was repetition and elaboration rather than fresh creation. Only in architecture did the new empire excel the old.

There was also something exceedingly wise in the political order. The three chief cities of the new realm — Chichen Itza, Uxmal, and Mayapan — formed a league whereby each was to share equally in the government of the empire. This triple alliance of powerful city-states kept the peace which enabled prosperity and arts and learning to flourish throughout the realm.

The Maya League was formed at the easily remembered date of 1000 A.D. It is interesting to view these happenings in Yucatan against events that were taking place elsewhere in world history at the same period. In the very year the Maya League was formed, Ericson was sailing from the Scandinavian countries to discover the continent on which the Maya were building a new empire. Only a little later (in 1066) William the Conqueror

Section of the Palace of the Governor of Uxmal, Yucatan

defeated Harold and introduced the new blood and new ideas
from which the high civilization of England began to rise.
Rome had long since been conquered by the rude tribes of
northern Europe, the Gauls and Goths, progenitors of the
French and Germans. With the decline of the classic civilizations, Europe was in the dark ages. Not even the first stirrings —
the early Gothic cathedrals, the guilds of scholars, the revival of
interest in classic art and learning — had begun to herald the
coming Renaissance. The idealism of Judea had long been

submerged by conquest, and the descendants of the prophets
and priests were scattered and persecuted. The Christian
Church had become an oppressive power rather than an inspiration. In China — at the other side of the earth — the
glorious Tang dynasty had ended. After the surge of art and
ideas under Buddhism, the lyric poetry of Li Po and his fellows,
the high era of learning led by the academies and the printing
press, China's greatness had swiftly ebbed. With the Orient in
a decline and Europe not yet stirring toward its future greatness,
the little Maya cities were for a brief period probably the most
brilliant centers of art and learning in the world.

The triple alliance, which kept the peace and opened the way
for prosperity and culture throughout Mayaland for nearly two
hundred years, was abruptly ended in 1194. The ruler of Chichen Itza plotted against the chief of Mayapan and, in the war
that followed, Mayapan, with the aid of allies called in from
Mexico, utterly routed the Itzan ruler and drove him from his
city. The Itza, however, did not easily accept defeat, and the
whole of the next century was full of their bloody efforts to
throw off the yoke of Mayapan. The following century was
marked by arrogance and oppression on the part of the rulers of
Mayapan, and by increasing cruelties from the Mexican soldiers
whom they imported in great numbers to keep their subjects in
check. At length Uxmal, which had held aloof from the strife,
joined the rebellion, and in the year 1441 a coalition under the
Lord of Uxmal was formed against the tyrannical rulers and
their foreign allies. Mayapan was attacked, captured, and
sacked.

With this battle the Maya seem to have spent the last of
their energies. All three of the cities of the original Maya League
were abandoned. Mayapan was destroyed. The Itza, dis-
couraged by the outlook, left Yucatan and founded a new

capital far to the south on an island in the Lake of Peten Itza. The leaders of Uxmal removed their capital to a point just south of old Mayapan and named their new city Mani, meaning 'it is finished.'

It was finished. The wars had exhausted the people and brought devastation to cities and lands. The country split into innumerable warring factions, each bent on the other's destruction. Presently there were added to the horrors of war three other calamities to make up the four dread horsemen of the Maya apocalypse. Following the wars came a great famine, then a sweeping pestilence. Then in 1517 the Spanish landed on the shores of Yucatan and soon set about the conquering of the country. Although the decimated and exhausted Maya fought valiantly, by 1541, foreign conquest, the last of the four destroying horsemen, had ridden with his killing hoofs over the prostrate body of what had been one of the world's great cultures.

THE AZTECS
OF MEXICO

THE AZTECS, who were building their civilization at about the time of the Maya renaissance, are the best known of the classic Indians. They were the dominant people of ancient Mexico, and relics of their temples and arts are eagerly studied by thousands of travelers every year. Descendants of the Aztecs, still speaking their own dialects, make up a million of the citizens of the present vigorous republic of Mexico, and Aztec blood is mixed in many other millions of modern Mexicans. Aztec words were taken over in large numbers by the Spanish colonists, and these words flavor all of Spanish-American speech. The Aztecs were also called the Mexica and their home became known as Mexico.

The Aztecs did not create a civilization. They simply took what others had created, organized it, and spread it to a wide group of people whom they conquered or with whom they carried on extensive trade. The relation of Aztec to Maya is strikingly similar to that of Rome to Greece. The Maya, like the Greeks, were the creators, the artists, the thinkers. The

Pottery from the Valley of Mexico

Aztecs, like the Romans, were the organizers, the administrators, the military power.

AZTEC HISTORY

By their own tradition, the Aztecs emerged from a mythical home in the north, the Seven Caves, at a time that would correspond with the year 800 A.D. in our calendar. No trace has been found of anything like the Seven Caves, but all evidence points to the fact that the Aztecs did come from the north. They were one of a number of related tribes who spoke a tongue called Nahua, a branch of the Shoshonean group of languages which is still spoken by Indians as far north as Montana and Oregon.

Many earlier groups had been active in the region which we know as Mexico. Among these, tradition gives a high place to the Toltecs who were also a Nahua-speaking people, probably

Pottery from Oaxaca

distant cousins of the Aztecs. It is hard to separate romantic
stories from accurate fact in the early history of Mexico, and
present scholars are suspicious of the tales of Toltec greatness
which were current in Aztec legend. At any rate, the early
Spanish chroniclers and the Indian scholars who wrote Mexican
history speak of the Toltecs as the fathers of civilization, partic-
ularly as the people who brought the learning and culture of the
Maya into Mexico. The word 'Toltec' means skilled worker.
The Toltecs, according to early accounts, were both skilled and
full of initiative — an artistic, imaginative, restless people.
They had begun to grow corn, to build temples, and to study
mathematics and astronomy long before the Aztecs arrived in
Mexico. They are reported to have been the people who went
into Yucatan to help Mayapan subdue the rival Maya cities.
They are supposed to have helped rebuild Chichen Itza and to
have learned a great deal of the science, religion, art, and agri-

culture which the Maya had developed to so high a point. Another early people of high talents were the Zapotecs who lived
in southern Mexico near Yucatan and who were probably
greatly influenced by the culture of the Maya.

Into the fertile region of Mexico, already occupied by
many earlier groups, a number of tribes of Nahua-speaking
people moved down from the north. The last of these, the
Aztecs, came into the broad high valley of Mexico, perhaps
about the middle of the eleventh century, and wandered un-
welcome for many years among the people who had come before
them. The first village which the Aztecs built for themselves, a
miserable group of grass huts in the swamps of Lake Tezcoco in
1325, became the foundation of their capital, Tenochtitlan,
which in turn grew into the stone-built city of Mexico.

Having gained a foothold through their little city in the
swamps, the Aztecs began at once to organize and fight. They
made their city into an island fortress and from it sent out raiding parties against neighboring cities. Within a hundred years
of their first settlement by the lake, they had become a strong
power and in 1437 they made their position secure by forming
an alliance with the neighboring cities of Tezcoco, just across
the lake, and Tlacopan, which stood a few miles to the west.
This partnership, known as the Aztec League, grew to be the
dominant force of the region. It held together firmly throughout the following century, each city sharing in the wars and spoils
of conquest and sharing also in the art and learning and state-
craft. The empire and the civilization which grew up around it
were the creation not of Mexico City alone but of the Aztec union.

The League at once gained power and prestige through the
forceful leadership of the King of Tezcoco and later through the
statesmanship of Montezuma the First, who came to the throne
of Mexico just after the alliance was formed. The brilliant rule

of this monarch, from 1440 to 1469, has earned for him the title
of Montezuma the Great. He made Mexico the dominant force
in the League and through a series of successful wars subdued a
great part of the surrounding country which he built into something approaching an empire.

During the century following the formation of the League,
the Aztec domain grew swiftly until it included much of the
huge territory which forms the present country of Mexico,
stretching east to the hot lowlands of the Atlantic and south to
Oaxaca and the Pacific. Less progress was made against the
fierce tribes of the western highlands, and the Empire was unable to extend its rule very effectively into the northern provinces. The monarchs who succeeded the first Montezuma continued to conquer the neighboring people and exact heavy
tribute from them, but it took constant warfare to collect the
taxes, and the territory was never organized into a unified nation. The fierce mountaineers of Tlascala, for example, less than
a hundred miles away, never were conquered. Many other
nations, while they bowed to superior force and paid tribute
more or less regularly, never thought of themselves as members
of the Aztec state; they sullenly waited for the time when they
could throw off the yoke of what they continued to regard as a
foreign power. Finally under the weak and vainglorious rule of
Montezuma the Second, a grand-nephew of the early statesman
of that name, the Empire collapsed before the force of the
Spanish conquest.

ARTS AND RELIGION

Aztec civilization was largely an extension of the culture of
the Maya and their neighbors. The Aztecs built magnificent
temples, developed an abundant agriculture, and created
beautiful works of art which even in their present ruins are im-

· Maguey plant, 'the friend of the poor'

pressive, but, except for details, these were not original. Many
features of the Maya calendar, the Maya number system, Maya
farming, and Maya art — together with additions and refine-
ments by the Toltecs and other intermediate people — were
taken over by the Aztecs.

Most of the people of ancient Mexico lived a peaceful routine
of farming and home arts. The crafts of spinning and weaving,
of pottery making and skilled work with leather and precious
metals were carried on much as they were among the Maya.
Maize was the staff of life, supplemented by a somewhat wider
variety of vegetables than was known in Central America or
Yucatan. One plant held so large a place in Mexican life that
it was known as 'the friend of the poor.' This was the agave or
maguey, commonly known in America as the century plant.
Its clustering pyramids of flowers covered the table lands with
beauty. Its leaves furnished thatch for roofing houses. From
its tough fibers, much like hemp, a strong thread was made
which was used even more than cotton in weaving cloth. The

thorns at the ends of the leaves were used for pins and needles. Its roots were cooked into a nourishing food. Its juice was fermented into a strong beverage, pulque, then as now the national drink of Mexico. Finally from its leaves was made the paper used for painting and picture writing.

The Aztec gods were even more numerous and grotesque than those of the Maya. One of them, Quetzalcoatl, was none other than the feathered serpent called Kukulcan by the Maya. In the myths of the Aztecs, as in those of the Maya, this plumed serpent was a human hero before he became divine, and with both peoples this feathered god was the favorite subject for sculpture and temple decorations.

The chief of the Aztec gods, however, was Huitzilopochtli, the terrible god of war. The Aztec religion was more formal and much more cruel than that of the earlier people. The devouring god of war was the symbol of the state, and his cruelty and thirst for blood saturated the state religion.

The Aztecs were as much interested in observing the movements of the heavenly bodies as the Maya were, and both these peoples studied the stars and charted a calendar for the glory of the gods. Through the study of the days and seasons the priests believed they could tell which times were favorable for planting and reaping, for starting a journey, or for making a war. The priests were a large and powerful class. It is recorded that five thousand priests and attendants served the single temple of the god of war in Mexico City.

A number of religious practices were strikingly similar to those followed by Christian churches. Children were baptized by having holy water sprinkled on their heads by priests. Confession of sins was regularly practised in the temples. A gesture was used in approaching the gods much like the Catholic practice of making the sign of the cross and bending the knee.

The Aztec worshipper, on entering the presence of a god, stooped, touched a finger to the earth, and then placed this finger upon his lips. This was known as 'eating dirt in homage to the gods.' The same gesture was used in saluting the monarch or any high lord, and it was also used as a form of oath or pledge of honor and truth. A communion service was held through the eating of little cakes made in the shape of the idols and blessed by the priests. Eating the flesh of victims who had been sacrificed to the gods was also thought of as communion; the strength of the victim and the spirit of the god were believed to enter the person who ate of the offering.

WAR AND COMMERCE

Almost equal to the priesthood in interest and prestige were two other professions: war and commerce.

It was natural that a state bent upon conquest should give a high place to the army. With the Aztecs, conquest was a driving

Worshipper 'eating dirt in homage to the gods'

Huitzilopochtli, the god of war

ambition, war a business. War was even a part of Mexican religion, for the priests demanded sacrifices of human victims in behalf of their gods, and only by the capture of war prisoners could victims be furnished in the numbers required. Military training was a large part of the education of the young, and service in the army was a career to which boys looked forward eagerly and proudly.

War in ancient Mexico was much more of a sporting event than it is in the modern world. Like all important acts in classic America, it was hedged about by ceremony and decorum. No battle was fought until messengers had notified the given city that an attack was to be made on a definitely named day. Sometimes battles were fought on fields specially laid out for

Warrior dressed in jaguar skin

the purpose, much as gladiatorial combats or football contests are held in certain fields on definite dates. The war was opened with offerings to the gods by both armies, and the first engagement was usually a ceremonial sham battle between specially designated corps. After these preliminaries, the armies fought valiantly and furiously, using ambush and sudden raids as well as the steady clash of spears and arrows to overcome the enemy. But victory was often determined by points of vantage gained rather than by the number of the slain and wounded. And since one of the prizes of triumph was a multitude of prisoners, there was little slaughter on the battlefield.

Trade was also a profession of great prestige. Contrary to the almost universal rule among early peoples, the Mexicans were devoted to commerce. In fact, Aztec influence spread quite as much by trade as by conquest, and the two were closely linked together. Whenever a new city was added to the Empire, the traders swarmed in. And merchants traveling to distant parts were under the special protection of the state. If they were robbed or were not given the freedom and hospitality they demanded, the army swooped down to punish the offenders and often remained to subdue and annex the city. Probably no people until the modern British ever used trade so successfully as a means of empire building.

Merchants were a high caste in Mexico. After successful trading exploits, they were allowed to carry a special staff, a symbol of commercial nobility. With huge caravans of porters carrying their goods, merchants traveled hundreds of miles, often being absent on their tours for more than a year. They spread every article of agriculture and of art and craft over the whole region of Mexico. They circulated knowledge and ideas. They caused highways to be built, which in turn stimulated movement and communication. Through this active commerce, for the first time in native American history, a common standard of living and common knowledge began to be spread over a wide domain.

A system of law courts grew up chiefly with a view to stabilizing and standardizing commerce. Judges acted upon crime and civil disputes in Mexico City and throughout the realm. While laws were not thoroughly codified, there was substantial uniformity in practice because of a centralized system of judges headed by a supreme judge who had the power of final

Aztec market place

review — much as the Supreme Court in the United States —
and whose decision could not be overruled even by the emperor.

Trade, as among most early people, was largely based on the
exchange of one article for another. But the Aztecs used also
an elementary form of money: little pieces of bronze cut into
the form of a T and specially designed bits of cotton cloth. The
lowest items of currency were cocoa beans, little sacks of them
being made up with fixed numbers of beans. An Aztec slang
expression was, 'I do not care for you even as much as two cocoa
beans,' as we might say, 'I don't care tuppence.' The highest
coins were little transparent quills filled with grains of gold —
an early recognition in America of the gold standard.

Naturally the commerce of the Empire centered in Mexico,

the capital. A great plaza of the city was devoted to the public mart. Special market days were held at five-day intervals and on these days the public square was a bedlam of activity. It is reported that more than forty thousand people from leagues around came to these markets.

Here are some of the craftsmen and their wares which the early chroniclers report that they saw in the great market place of Mexico: goldsmiths from Atzcapozalco, potters and jewelers from Cholula, painters from Tezcoco, hunters from the highlands, fishermen from far distant rivers and lakes, stonecutters, weavers, venders of fruits and flowers. Cotton was piled in bales or woven into cloth and made into dresses and tapestries. Booth after booth was lined with vases of clay or carved wood. Hatchets and swords with copper edges were on display, and quilted doublets to be used as armour, made of cotton sometimes coated with feathers; knives and mirrors made of obsidian, a natural glass of the region; ornaments and trinkets of all sorts, including toy birds made of precious metals with feathers alternately of gold and silver and with movable heads and bodies. There were drugs made from roots and herbs; blank books, folded together like fans, made sometimes of cotton or skins but usually of agave; hides and leather goods; wild animals and hundreds of turkeys. Also in special stands were pots of chocolate, steaming and savory, intoxicating drinks, *ahuacotl*, or avocado pears, bread and cakes made from Indian corn. Every stall and portico was decked with flowers which grew in rich profusion in the Valley of Mexico. Building materials were also on sale: stone, lime, and timber. And there was a considerable commerce in slaves.

Oddly enough with all this trade, weights or scales seem never to have been invented or used by the Mexicans. Everything was sold by count or size, and quality rather than quantity seems to have been given much more consideration by the Mexican traders than it is in modern commerce.

Good order ruled in the Mexican market. Police patrolled the square but were seldom needed. A court of twelve judges sat in the market place and promptly settled any dispute, having full authority even to give the death penalty in case of theft.

THE AZTEC CAPITAL

The center of the Aztec Empire, not only in commerce but in all things, was Tenochtitlan or Mexico, the capital city. From the little group of mud and thatch huts in the swamps which the Aztecs first built, it grew to be probably the finest city in all native America, the city built upon the lake, the Venice of the West.

The site of Mexico City was and is to this day one of the most beautiful in the world. It stands in the center of the great Valley of Mexico, a huge saucer two hundred miles around, resting on a high plateau a mile and a half above the level of the sea. The huge valley is rimmed by great mountain peaks rising as high as 17,852 feet, among which stand as everlasting sentinels the two famous volcanoes: Popocatepetl, 'the mountain that smokes,' and Iztaccihuatl, 'the woman in white.' In Aztec days this high valley was a mosaic of water, woodland, and cultivated plains, dotted here and there with the white stone of city temples and palaces and the earth and thatch of village homes.

Tenochtitlan, built well out into the waters of Lake Tezcoco, was connected with the shore by great dikes or roadways of stone and cement wide enough, as the early Spaniards reported, for ten or twelve men to ride abreast. Drawbridges on these dikes could be pulled up to cut off the approach of enemies and thus make of the city an almost impregnable island fortress.

Floating on Lake Tezcoco were the chinampas, wandering islands

Floating about on the broad shallow waters of the lake were the weird and romantic *chinampas*, floating islands. On these wandering islands, made of rafts covered with earth, the farmers raised their maize and vegetables and often built their huts. It is said these floating farms were invented by the Aztecs in the early days when, driven from the surrounding land by fierce and jealous neighbors, they had to find some means of raising food within the confines of their swampy lake. These wandering gardens, often two or three hundred feet in length and bordered by rows of gay flowers, were pushed about the waters by long poles. Thus farmers could let their crops grow in some sheltered nook, then sail the whole farm to market or to any place they pleased about the lake.

The founders of Mexico built their first frail tenements of reeds and thatch on a group of small islands in the western elbow of the lake. But as the city grew, long poles were driven into the marshes and, on these firm piles, wooden houses were built, standing over the water as if on stilts. Later, light brittle stone from near-by quarries furnished the materials for the larger homes and for the palaces and temples.

One wide avenue, with low stone houses and terraced gardens, swept straight through the city. Other streets alternated with canals and wide waterways which served as chief avenues for the city's traffic. Embankments of hard earth or cement were built along the sides of many of the canals to serve as footpaths and landing places for the myriads of canoes and rafts which plied these waterways. The same boats which served the canals of the city carried on a busy commerce with the other towns and villages of this inland sea.

With a population of three hundred thousand (as estimated from the sixty thousand houses found by the Spaniards), an efficient city management was necessary. Water was brought in by great earthen pipes laid along a causeway from the fresh springs of Chapultepec, 'the hill of grasshoppers,' about three miles away. A careful police concerned themselves chiefly with health and cleanliness since crime and disorder were held in check by public opinion and an almost universally accepted code of conduct. A thousand persons daily swept and watered the streets, and each householder was expected to keep his home whitewashed without and clean within. Burning braziers lighted the principal streets throughout the night.

The central feature of the Aztec capital was the magnificent temple plaza, called *tecpan*, which stood on the same site as the present cathedral square of modern Mexico City. The old plaza was enclosed by a wall of stone and lime about eight feet high and so ornamented with carved figures of serpents that it was known as the serpent wall. Fray Sahagun, one of the early Spanish priests whose manuscript histories tell of Aztec life at the time of the conquest, reports that within the temple plaza stood twenty-five temple pyramids and scores of priests' houses, feasting pavilions, ball courts, dancing halls, and arsenals. Within this sacred square were two other peculiar sights: a mammoth cage for idols taken from conquered cities, a kind of prison for alien gods, and a series of huge racks on which were arranged the thousands of skulls of victims who had been sacrificed on the altars.

The crowning structure of the temple plaza was the great pyramid, *teocalli*, or place of the gods. The pyramid was built of earth and pebbles and covered with hewn stone. It did not run up to a point as the pyramids of Egypt do, but, like all Indian pyramids, was cut off about half way up. The flat area on the top of the truncated pyramid served as a platform for the shrines. Before each of the two temples of the great *teocalli* stood an altar with a fire constantly burning upon it. In the center of the platform, before the temples, lay a solid block of jasper on which human victims were slain and offered as sacrifices to the gods. Here also was the huge drum of serpent skins, struck only on special occasions and giving out a low melancholy boom that could be heard for miles. Flights of stairs were built up the outside walls so that in order to reach the top of the pyramid it was necessary to make a complete circle of it. This gave a dramatic effect to religious ceremonies, with processions of costumed priests climbing upward to the blare of wild music, with scores of human victims being led to the sacrifice, all winding round and round and up and up to the temples and the altars.

Many of the majestic objects of Aztec art were created as decorations for the various temples of the sacred square, such, for example, as the great Calendar Stone or Stone of the Sun. This monument, in the shape of a circle twelve feet across, was quarried in a single slab of porphyry weighing originally some fifty tons and dragged over many miles of marshy lake to be set

The great Calendar Stone or Stone of the Sun

up before the Temple of the Sun. The stone is a remarkable example of Aztec carving. In addition to a central symbol of the sun's face marked with the divisions of the calendar, it records in picture writing the whole long Aztec myth of the creations and destructions of the world.

Imposing squares were formed by the palaces of the emperor and the courts set aside for visiting nobles. The splendor of Montezuma's palace amazed the Spanish invaders with its rooms so huge that certain of them could hold a thousand men, with its rafters of cedar, its rich draperies, its ornaments of precious stones, its furnishings of Cholula pottery and of gold; its charming courtyards and flower gardens; its plazas for the exhibition of animals and birds collected from all parts of the kingdom.

AZTEC NEIGHBORS

Mexico was not the only important city of the realm. Aztec civilization was made up of contributions from many cities and many peoples. Cholula, a city seventy-five miles southeast of Mexico, near the present site of Puebla, was famous for its art and its shrines. In this beautiful city, tradition said, Quetzalcoatl had lived for twenty years as a man, long before he became a god, and had taught the inhabitants the arts of civilization and the beauties of a religion which used only fruits and flowers as offerings and which taught that 'the Kingdom of Heaven is within you.' In honor of this divine hero, there stands to this day the ruins of the great 'mound of Cholula,' a huge pyramid originally 177 feet high with a base 1423 feet long — twice as long as the great Egyptian pyramid of Cheops — covering an area of 44 acres at the base and having at its top an earth platform of more than an acre on which stood the temple to Quetzalcoatl, the feathered serpent, the god of the air. Cholula was the holy city of the Mexican realm. Many tribes kept the temples of their own gods there and came on pilgrimages from miles around. Worship of tribal gods went on in two hundred temples throughout the city, while high above all towered the great pyramid with its temple to Quetzalcoatl, with its mystic promise that the divine hero would some day return to save and glorify his people.

Chief cities of the Toltecs were Teotihuacan, 'Where the gods dwell' (famous for the great pyramids to the Sun and the Moon and a picturesque roadway lined with small pyramids called

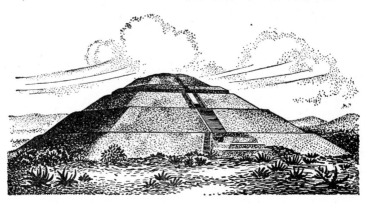

Pyramid of the Sun in the Toltec city of Teotihuacan

the Pathway of the Dead); and Tula, where modern students are finding beautiful examples of architecture and carving, especially a number of sculptured columns in the form of feathered serpents and gigantic human figures. Monte Alban, far to the south, overlooking the modern city of Oaxaca, was a chief center of the Zapotecs. Relics from these ancient cities show the paths and peoples through which the art and learning of the earlier Maya cities were carried into Mexico.

One of the cities which was a partner in the Aztec League — Tezcoco, which stood just across the shallow lake from Mexico — was for a time of great importance. There, as a friendly neighbor of Montezuma the Great, lived a picturesque statesman, Nezahualcoyotl. This name, which means 'Hungry Coyote,' was probably taken by the monarch in memory of the years of his youth when, in danger of his life, he roamed the countryside like a hunted animal. When he was a lad of fifteen, fierce enemies from the north attacked Tezcoco, conquered it, and butchered the king, his father, before his eyes. The young prince fled and for nearly a decade hid in caves and forests to escape his conquerors.

The life of Hungry Coyote was recorded in great detail and probably with some flights of romantic fancy by a great grandson. The manuscripts of this Indian scholar are the source of much of our knowledge not only of this monarch but of many items of early Mexican history.

The story is full of hair-raising escapes by the young prince during his early years and of the wisdom and glory of his later reign. Once he hid from his pursuers in a great drum about which his friends loyally continued to dance. Another time, as he was fleeing from an armed band, a girl reaping in the fields buried him under the huge stalks she was gathering. Once, surrounded in a temple, he hid himself behind the billowing smoke of the incense of burning gum. In many ways the early life of Hungry Coyote reminds one of the privations of David as a shepherd on the hills of Judea or fleeing from the jealous wrath of King Saul. And the later life of this Mexican monarch also follows the story of King David, for each was a mighty warrior, a mystic man of God, a pioneer builder of a rude kingdom, and a poet. Even in love these two chieftains had a striking similarity: the Mexican got his beautiful dark bride by having her spouse sent into the front line of battle and killed by the fierce Tlascalans, just as David took Bathsheba after having her husband, Uriah, slain in the war against the Ammonites.

In the course of time Hungry Coyote was able to rally his loyal followers and, gaining the aid of the city of Mexico, led an army which routed his enemies and re-established his kingdom. Since victory had so happily followed this alliance of Tezcoco and Mexico, these cities decided to add the neighboring little kingdom of Tlacopan to their group and form a League of Nations of the Valley of Mexico. Hungry Coyote was therefore the leading factor in building the Aztec League, though his influence was later surpassed by that of Montezuma the Great, and his state took a place second to the aggressive city of Mexico.

Restored to his throne, Hungry Coyote proceeded to build a united country. His armies added territory rapidly to Tezcoco and thus to the domain of the Aztec League. He issued a code of laws and appointed judges to carry them out. He took a great interest in religion. He sought for better administration by dividing the burden of government among a number of departments, appointing councils of war, finance, and justice. He created one other agency, unusual among government departments, the Council of Music, which served as a general academy of art and learning. Works on astronomy or history had to be presented to this Council before they were made public. It supervised the arts and crafts. It appointed teachers of the young and set examinations. To membership in this academy were appointed those who were thought to be the wisest men of the kingdom and with these wise men sat the monarchs of the three states of the Aztec League.

Among the most illustrious of the singers who appeared before this academy was the man who created it. Many of the psalms of the King of Tezcoco are recorded in the manuscripts of his historian. While impossible in another tongue to give the poetic form, the following rather literal translation into English of a few stanzas will give some idea of the poetry of this royal bard:

> Banish care. If there be bounds to pleasure, the saddest life must also have an end. Then weave your wreath of flowers, and sing your songs in praise of the all-powerful God; for the glory of this world soon fades away. Rejoice in the green freshness of your spring; for the day will come when you shall sigh for these joys in vain; when the sceptre shall pass from your hands, your servants shall wander desolate in your courts, your sons, and the sons of your nobles, shall drink the dregs of sorrow, and all the

pomp of your victories and triumphs shall live only in their recollection. Yet the remembrance of the just shall not pass away from the nations, and the good you have done shall ever be held in honor.

FLASHES FROM AZTEC LIFE

Life for the average countryman in ancient Mexico must have been a dull routine of laborious farming with few comforts and conveniences and with a low level of subsistence. Women worked all day long at household tasks of tedious hand labor and back-breaking drudgery. A part of the hard-earned crops had to go for taxes or tribute. Children began to help in farm and home labor as soon as they could walk. Hard work throughout the years and a meager, uncomfortable living made up the round for the masses.

But life in the Mexican capital was full of pomp and drama. The monarch held court for his nobles — including the noble merchants — and for the visiting kings and courtiers from the allied and subject cities. The army displayed its prowess in frequent exhibitions, and the generals plotted with traveling merchants about incidents which might be used as the excuse for further conquest. The young people of good family went to schools, which were numerous and well organized and which emphasized deportment and manners as well as special training in religion and war for the boys and in the hand crafts and home arts for the girls.

The great American passion for playing ball has ancient and honorable ancestry on the continent. The particular game which fascinated the Aztecs (and also the Toltecs and Maya) was a kind of basketball, called *tlachtli*, played with a solid ball of rubber hurled or bounced not by the hands or feet but by the hips and knees. In connection with many of the temples was a sacred ball court, beautifully designed and richly decorated, with a stone ring built into the masonry at the center of each of the two side walls. The object of the game was to get the ball through the ring but since the ball was a heavy mass of crude native rubber which could be knocked about only by the buttocks and the knees, it was not often that a goal was made. When it did happen, bedlam broke loose. The man scoring a ring not only won the contest but immediately became a public idol. Incidentally, he won the clothing and ornaments of the spectators. In the thrilling event of a goal, the audience jumped up for one wild cheer, then dashed madly for the gates, trying to escape before the victor or his friends could seize them and tear off their clothes. At these games the spectators were literally liable to lose their shirts. Professionals played before tense audiences. Amateurs counted skill in the ball game among their highest honors. Games were played for high stakes, men often gambling themselves into slavery on the outcome of their play.

The chief centers of interest were the temples and the temple ceremonies. Mexico was said to have had more than a thousand shrines, and before each of the sacred altars priests were almost continuously, day and night, performing services, tending the eternal fires, directing sacred rituals and pageants. The Aztec calendar grew to be a succession of saints' days, periods set aside for ceremonies to the numerous gods. And religion, under the aegis of the cruel god of war, came to be a series of penances and sacrifices.

Worshippers cut their ears and tongues with sharp maguey thorns and poured their blood over the images. Human sacrifice became not so much a rite as an obsession. Wars were often fought chiefly for the purpose of getting hordes of captives to offer to the gods who came to be thought of as depending on human blood for their lives. Each emperor, before he took office, was required to conduct a war party and bring home

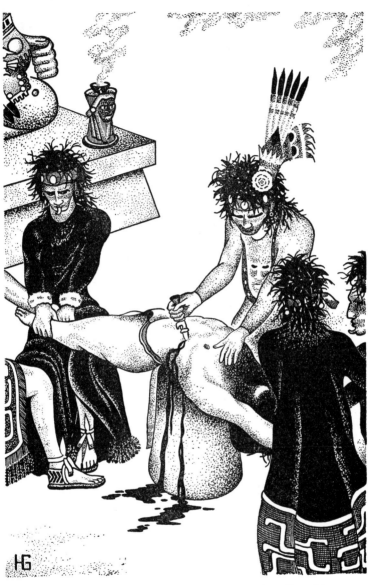

Religion among the Aztecs came to be a series of sacrifices

victims to be slain at his coronation so that the gods would bless
his reign. An Aztec stone carving reports that at the dedication
of one of the temples 20,000 prisoners of war were sacrificed.
While this may be a gross exaggeration, it gives an idea of the
customs. Babies were sacrificed at planting time. It was a good
omen for them to cry, for their many tears promised abundant
rains. While in general the Aztecs were a cleanly people, being
devoted to sweat baths as well as to less violent washings, there
was a sacred rule that priests could never wash their heads nor
cut nor comb their hair. Since it was good form for much blood
to splash over the priests at the sacrifices, the state of their hair
became frightful; 'the odor of sanctity' took on a literal meaning.

The ceremonies were full of color and pageantry. In the
Aztec maize dance, virgins carried the seed corn to the temple
of the god of grain that it might be blessed, marching in solemn
procession, their arms and legs clothed with red feathers and
their faces smeared with black wax. In certain ceremonies to
the goddesses, men and women danced together hand in hand
or with arms about each other's shoulders. In others, women
pelted each other with garlands of leaves and flowers or were
pummeled by men and boys who carried little bags tied to the
end of long cords.

Even the sacrifices had picturesque features. The annual
feast to the god Yautl, for example, included the killing of
a young man who, so to speak, had been fattened for the sacrifice. Fray Sahagun reports in his chronicles that 'a youth of
handsome body and polished disposition' was chosen on the day
sacred to Yautl and for the whole of the year he was given every
privilege and pleasure, being treated as if he were himself the
god. He was dressed in robes rich and bizarre, for the Aztecs
always thought of their gods as grotesque in appearance.
Every day fresh garlands of flowers were hung about his neck,

much like the flower leis of Hawaii. To his legs were tied rattles and jingles which made a merry noise as he walked about. He was fed on the finest foods and taught the most elegant graces, including playing on the flute and smoking tobacco. During the whole of the year this sacred dandy wandered about the streets, attended by eight holy pages, playing on his flutes, puffing on his little carved pipes, and smelling sweet flowers. During the last month he was given for his further enjoyment four sacred virgins who had been chosen for their beauty and grace and had also been kept in a year's special luxury for this rôle.

When the full cycle of the year was complete and the day of Yautl came round, the young man walked up the steps of the pyramid sacred to this god, playing his flutes while the populace watched and thrilled. Coming to the temple at the top of the pyramid, he was seized by the waiting priests who plunged their stone knives into his breast, tore out his heart, presented it to the sun, and then promptly went about choosing another young man to play Yautl for the coming year.

The most spectacular ceremony of the calendar was the 'tying up of the seasons' at the conclusion of the great cycle of fifty-two years. By the complex counting of days which the Aztecs used, the same day-name and number count came together only once in fifty-two years (somewhat as in our calendar Friday the thirteenth occurs infrequently). The end of the calendar cycle came at exactly the mid-point of the intricate swing through the heavens of the planet Venus. The Aztecs came to regard these cycles as of fateful moment. They feared the world might come to an end at the conclusion of each of these eras. It was a matter of world salvation to get the new cycle started. Hence the custom of renewing the fires and 'binding the years.'

The high priest kindles the new fire

Just before the closing hour of the fifty-two-year period, all fires were allowed to die — even the sacred fires in the temples which, with the greatest care, were kept burning 'eternally' during the cycle. Believing that time would continue and the world go on only if the gods showed their favor by allowing the fires to be rekindled, the season toward the close of the cycle was devoted to special efforts to appease the gods. All idols, both in the temples and in private homes, were replaced. The braziers and furnishings of the temples were renewed. All buildings were whitewashed and renovated.

At sunset of the fateful evening, the priests in special gorgeous robes set out for a sacred hill about three miles from the city of Mexico. The procession, which included a large part of the populace, was timed to reach the hill just before midnight. Meanwhile, not only in the capital city but throughout the length and breadth of the land, every fire in home and temple had died out. Hushed, terrified, thrilled, the people waited to see if fire could be rekindled, if the world would go on. At exactly midnight, the high priest, amid the greatest suspense, kindled the new fire by the time-honored method of twirling a stout stick on a board of softer wood. At the first whisk of flame, a shout of joy arose from the populace. Immediately a great bonfire was lit from the newly kindled fire so that the people for miles around might know that the gods were favorable and that time would march on. Runners dipped pine torches in the new fire and sped forth to their villages. Fresh runners, placed along the path, caught up the divine fire and raced with it to the remotest parts of the country. The early chroniclers say that night was as bright as day from the multitude of torches rushing in all directions carrying new life throughout the realm.

SPANISH CONQUEST

During nearly a century the Aztec League flourished under the leadership of Mexico, developing a well-balanced civilization of agriculture, trade, arts, and religion. While the Empire was a loose confederation of allies and subject peoples rather than a unified nation, steady progress was being made toward common life and common government for a whole great realm. Then suddenly the Spanish conquest struck its shattering blow and the natural course of Mexican history was broken.

It is one of the amazing events of history that Cortez and his few hundred soldiers were able to conquer the strong and warloving Empire of the Aztecs. A united resistance by the Indians would have routed the invading army quickly and utterly. While Cortez was a shrewd and brave general, it was strife and weakness within the Empire that gave the Spaniards their victory.

It was a fateful misfortune that the second Montezuma, a

grand-nephew of Montezuma the Great, was chief of the Aztec state when the Spaniards arrived. The younger Montezuma, in unhappy contrast to his wise and vigorous predecessors, was a vain despot. His arrogance had weakened his government, angered his subjects, and alienated his allies. Surprised and confused by the sudden arrival of the Spanish in 1519, Montezuma hesitated and wavered while his enemies joined forces with the invaders and his allies held aloof.

To the Indians, the Spaniards with their strange and powerful weapons seemed possessed of magic, and the coming of the fair

Montezuma

and bearded strangers appeared to be the fulfillment of the old prophesy of the return of Quetzalcoatl. Fear and superstition weakened resistance. Horses, never seen in America until the Spaniards came, were terrifying. To the Indians the horsemen seemed weird centaurs — devils who could cut themselves in two, one half walking on two legs, the other prancing about on four. And Cortez was clever enough to play upon the jealousy of rival cities and to persuade many of the fierce neighbors of the Aztecs to join him in attacking Montezuma and overthrowing the Empire. Accustomed to thinking of war as a kind of game in the struggle for power, Tlascala and other states eagerly joined the Spanish invaders in the exciting adventure of attacking the Aztec capital.

The invaders came not only with strong arms and clever strategy; they came burning with greed and intolerance. They had such lust for power that no suffering was too great for them to endure, no treachery or brutality too despicable for them to use. They had such madness for gold that they carried off all they could get their hands on, laying waste beautiful cities, rifling graves, tearing asunder priceless jewels and monuments. They were so intolerant that they stamped out everything they could of native life, native religion, and native art. They burned the books of painted picture writing, declaring that they were full of the works of the devil; they tore down the magnificent stone and stucco temples and used the materials to build fortresses and churches for themselves; they broke up the statuary, smashed the carvings, and destroyed the stone tablets of calendar records in a pious zeal 'to free the benighted people from their pagan lore.'

They not only destroyed the material culture, but they so broke the spirit of the people and so firmly planted the idea of native inferiority that for four centuries the world has largely accepted the statement that the Spanish conquest was a triumph of civilization over barbarism. No enlightened person believes that today. Anyone who studies the relics and records that have survived must recognize that in Mexico the Europeans crushed a vigorous empire and shattered beyond repair a noble civilization.

THE INCA EMPIRE
OF PERU

THE INCA EMPIRE had its center at Cuzco on the highlands of
Peru. It was the largest of the Indian domains — one of the
great empires of all history — and was a thoroughly organized
and unified nation, not like the loosely grouped city-states of
the Maya or the confederation under the Aztecs. Inca culture
began to flower during the latter part of the Maya renaissance
at about the time that the Aztecs were first gaining a foothold in
Mexico. Doubtless influences from Central America played a
part in both the agriculture and the arts of Peru, but in the
main Inca culture was a distinct and independent growth.

The origin of the Incas was told in a widely accepted myth
as full of romance and picturesque detail as any of the Greek
or Norse legends. From caverns in the House of Dawn — so
the myth runs — four brothers set out to found the kingdom.
The eldest was Manco, the high priest of the Sun god from whom
the brothers claimed direct descent. The names of the other
brothers were words which in English are Salt, Pepper, and

Pleasure. Manco carried an emblem which directed the steps of the explorers in their search for the sacred spot on which they were to found their state and their church, and a golden divining rod which was to mark the end of the journey by sinking into the ground at the site of their destined home.

The journey was a veritable odyssey, teeming with adventures and perils, and in the course of it the three younger brothers were lured by evil spirits to their death. Salt was tempted to turn back to collect some trinkets in a sacred cave, and when he entered a great rock was rolled against the door, sealing his doom. Pepper, in trying to seize a stone statue, was himself turned to stone. The place where this miracle occurred was named Haunacauri and became a sacred spot in Incaland dedicated to boys just entering manhood. Pleasure, who was winged, flew up to the top of a mountain (afterward the site of the great Sun temple near Cuzco) and on alighting was so exhausted that he solidified into stone. Undaunted, Manco trudged on to the promised land and, at the spot where his golden rod finally sank into the earth, he founded the city of Cuzco, set up the worship of the Sun, and began the rule of the Saca Inca.[1]

The less romantic history is that, building on earlier cultures, a tribe or family known as the Inca slowly established a military power at the headwaters of the Ucayali River on the highlands of Peru. Thence they began to conquer the surrounding tribes by raids and later by well-organized military expeditions. In 1100 A.D. Sinchi Rocca, the first Inca ruler known to

[1] The use of the word Inca throughout the history of Peru is confusing. Originally it was simply the name of a family or tribe. Then as the Empire grew, members of the tribe, who were all relatives of the Emperor, were made nobles and were given the chief posts in the government and the priesthood. Thus Incas came to mean nobles. In its strictest sense, the name was used for the ruler who was called Saca Inca, which means the Only Inca. The word is also used to designate the whole Empire and the civilization which grew up under it.

sober history, took the throne. From that time on for four
hundred years the Empire steadily expanded its territory and
intensified its rule until the realm became known in native
speech as Tavantinsuyu, 'the four quarters of the world.'

Vigorous peoples had flourished in the region for hundreds
of years, notably the Chimu of the coastal plains, the Ti-
ahuanacans of the highlands, and the Chancas of the northern
woodlands. On these early cultures the Incas built their great
civilization. By steady conquest of the various peoples the
Incas created a mighty Empire which, by the year 1500,
extended from Quito in Ecuador to Tucuman, far south into
what is now Argentina. Many states did not have to be conquered but came voluntarily to join the great nation and share
in its benefits and its prestige. At the height of its power the
Inca Empire stretched for two thousand miles along the high
plateaus of the Andes and the coastal plains of the Pacific
Ocean. It covered 380,000 square miles, an area as great as
all the Atlantic seaboard states of America from Florida to
Maine, or the combined area of France and Spain. Its population has been variously reported; conservative estimates put it
around four million. This huge realm, made up of strong
and diverse people, was welded into a unified kingdom. An
enormous and efficient bureaucracy ruled the mighty Empire,
backed by powerful armies and supported even more strongly
by the awe and reverence which the whole people felt for the
Saca Inca.

INCA GOVERNMENT

Contrary to the native American custom, the rule of the Inca
was pure hereditary despotism. The Saca Inca was not only
ruler but god. He was the head of the priesthood, dictator of
the bureaucracy, and commander of the army. He made the

laws and appointed the judges and governors to enforce them.

The political order was state socialism, and the administration of every feature was carried out with efficient management and minute supervision. It is hard to imagine a more complete regimentation than the Incas achieved, though they were wise enough to soften their rule by some consideration for local custom, by privileges and bonuses granted to those who were called upon to do unusual tasks, and by a great number of holidays crammed with feasts and festivals to humor both the bodies and the souls of the people.

The whole great Empire was managed as a single economic unit. Food from the farms was distributed to the artisans, the road builders, the soldiers, and all other groups of workers. Fabrics from the various crafts were similarly distributed to all the people. Seed and fertilizer were often furnished by the state to the farmers, wool and cotton to the craftsmen, metals to the artisans. Roads and irrigation systems were built with a view to the public needs. The army was thought of as an instrument of the people — as well as of the monarchy — for adding new territory and thus supplying greater comforts. Soldiers were kept in check and were never allowed to trespass upon the villages and farms through which they marched or in any way to impose upon the people. Newly conquered provinces were not destroyed or exploited by heavy taxes but were brought as quickly as possible into the economy and benefits of the Empire.

For effective administration, the Empire was divided into provinces, each ruled by a governor called Curaso. Under the Curaso was a great series of officials ranging from regional governors to sub-chiefs who directed counties or hamlets and finally to petty officials who supervised groups of only ten families. Inca nobles served as heads of all important departments

Inca palace and nobles

in the central government in Cuzco and were often themselves
the provincial chiefs. On top, directing all and unifying all,
stood the Saca Inca, the absolute ruler.

Every newly acquired province was bound into the Empire
speedily and effectively. While the Empire grew steadily, it
was not built in haste. Its unity was achieved by the thorough
assimilation of each new territory. As a province was annexed,
fortresses and government offices were built. Even while the
army was still completing its conquest, a host of officials, road
builders, and artisans were rushed in. In each new province a
census of the population and an economic survey were among
the first tasks.

As a means both of preventing insurrection and of developing
the economy of the whole Empire, large blocks of the population

of new provinces were often moved to other regions. But the Incas were wise enough to temper these deportations with special benefits. The people were usually moved to regions similar in climate and farming conditions to those from which they were taken. During the period of adjustment they were allowed to use all their produce for their own consumption. They were favored in the distribution of clothes and other products of the crafts. But with a view to maintaining the strict division of labor and the economical distribution of population, no shifting around was permitted except on orders of the state. An individual born to a certain occupation in a given locality could neither change his trade, move from his village, nor marry outside his local group.

If the former ruler of any captured country was not too rebellious, he was retained as governor of the province, and the regional and village chiefs were kept on as well. Meanwhile, a member of the Inca nobility — a close relative of the Saca Inca — was moved in to serve as associate governor with power to veto unwise or rebellious acts. Another Inca was set up as high priest of the province, and a division of the army remained under a tried and loyal general. Thus, though power was completely in the hands of the Inca government, the conduct of daily affairs went on smoothly under the old rulers who knew the people and their ways. The heirs of the conquered ruler were brought to Cuzco where they were held as hostages for the good behavior of their father and at the same time were taught the principles of Inca government and steeped in the tradition and atmosphere of the Inca Empire.

Constant communications over the network of roads kept the Empire together. Each monarch began his reign by a grand tour of the whole realm and all sections were visited regularly by high officials who inspected activities and listened to complaints. If questions of importance came up they were referred to Cuzco, and federal judges were sent out to administer justice. But all routine law and petty offenses were handled by local courts. The rule of these efficient courts was that judgment in every case must be made within five days. Punishment was usually by flogging or death, fines being of small account where there was so little private property. Crime of any sort, however, seems to have been rare. This was partly because of the close and constant supervision, partly because the laws of the Inca — wisely very few though very strict — were regarded as divine commands, and partly because of the natural docility of the people. Furthermore, the Peruvian tradition was that the family and even the whole village was responsible for a man's acts and should share his punishment. This meant strong pressure on the individual to comply with the conventions lest harm come to the group around him.

In this realm, with its devotion to thrift and economic planning, the unforgivable sin was theft. Other crimes were rated in so far as they were thought to approach this most serious offense. One of the early monarchs, noted for his epigrams, is credited with these comments:

> Adulterers, who destroy the peace and happiness of others, should be declared thieves and condemned to death.

> Judges, who secretly receive gifts from suitors, ought to be looked upon as thieves and punished with death.

Inca law recognized two degrees of theft (just as we recognize varying degrees in our capital offense of murder): stealing with malice aforethought, which was punishable by death; and stealing from hunger or dire need, in which case the punishment was levied not against the thief but against the official who should have forestalled the need.

The realm was bound together by a common language. Most of the tribes of the region spoke dialects which were branches of a common tongue, and one of these dialects, Quichua, was made the official language of the whole Empire. Under Inca rule every inhabitant was obliged to learn and speak this tongue. The language was constantly enriched by taking in words and phrases from the various provinces and dialects. Poems and stories composed in this common tongue were recited throughout the Empire and created a feeling of unity among the whole people.

FARMING

The great industry was agriculture and, contrary to general Indian practice, farming in Peru was carried out intensively and with scientific planning. Every crop known to the Incas was cultivated in just those regions where it grew best. As a result there were rich harvests. The state directed the farming and to a great extent distributed the produce. Huge ware-houses in various parts of the realm kept surplus stores against times of famine or emergency. The general distribution was carried out with such care and equity that among the millions of this far-flung Empire there was little hunger or want.

This did not mean that the masses were well off. Even with the best planning subsistence was meager. The common people lived chiefly on maize, potatoes, and charqui (dried or 'jerked' meat of the llama), washed down by chicha, a native beer made from corn. There was none of the nourishing chocolate so widely used by the Maya and the Aztecs, but a kind of tea was brewed from leaves of maguey or mulli trees. The average house was a one-room rectangle with floors of trodden earth, without windows or chimneys. These huts, built of stones or stubble in the highlands and of adobe on the coastal plains, were shared with guinea pigs, dogs, fleas, and miscellaneous vermin.

The farm lands were worked co-operatively, part of the produce going to the state and the church and the remainder to the individual farmers who occupied the land. Every available bit of fertile ground was used. The mountain slopes were terraced by building walls of rough stone at intervals up the mountainsides and leveling off the ground behind them. These mountain fields, as well as the coastal deserts, were watered by an extensive irrigation system, the water being brought from springs high on the mountainside and carried from terrace to terrace so that one stream would serve a multitude of farms. It was a crime punishable by death to interfere in any way with the irrigation systems or to turn water from a neighbor's field into one's own farm.

Men dug up the earth; women followed breaking up clods and picking out weeds

In cultivating maize, the chief crop in Peru as elsewhere in America, the whole populace took a part. Each day the local overseer announced the fields which were to be worked. The men assembled with their digging sticks, long pointed stakes often with notches in the sides so that the foot might be used for driving the stick into the ground. Acting together to the lilt of a song, the army of farmers dug hills or furrows. Sometimes six or eight men would tie ropes to a digging stick and drag it along while one man held it in the ground — the nearest thing to a plow ever known in native America. The women followed to break up the clods and pick out the weeds. The crop was then sowed and the earth scraped back over the kernels, either with sticks, or, more often, just with the feet of the planters. Old people, children, and any persons too infirm to take part in active farming were stationed in the fields to drive birds away from the growing grain. While farming meant hard labor, it also meant a good deal of pleasure. Great numbers gathered for the communal tasks. It was a time for visiting and gossip. And chants and national songs carried the work along in a rhythmic swing.

A crop distinctive to Peru was the potato. Sweet potatoes were known in Central and North America but the white potato was found only around Peru. This staple spread around the world as soon as the Europeans discovered it and is now grown almost everywhere. It became such a basic food in Ireland that it is often called the Irish potato. Two other crops grown only in Peru until commerce spread them about the world were coca from which cocaine is made, and chinchona, the source of quinine. Most of the crops known in North America were also common to Peru. Beans and squashes, however, seem to have been less important than they were among the Maya and the Aztecs. And tobacco was not smoked or chewed but used only in snuff as a medicine.

The Incas developed one aspect of farming unknown elsewhere in native America. They were the only Indians who kept domestic animals. The highlands were filled with grazing herds of llamas, a small native species of wool-bearing camels, which were tended much as sheep are elsewhere, individual flocks sometimes running to thousands of heads. Two varieties of these animals were tamed and shepherded and two other varieties roamed wild in the mountains. Of the tame groups the alpaca had the finer wool, though the very choicest fleece, reserved exclusively for the costumes of the Inca, came from one of the wild groups, the vicuña. The common variety among the tamed herds, usually known simply by the general term llama, was almost as basic to the life of the people as maize. The llama furnished most of the wool used in textiles and a large part of the meat in the Peruvian diet. The llamas were also most useful as pack animals since they could forage from the most barren fields of moss and stunted herbs and could go for days and even weeks without water. And they were intimate companions and playmates of the people.

Fishing in the coastal regions and hunting in the highlands were well organized. Nets and harpoons are the fishing tools referred to in historical accounts, but pictures on vases show that hook and line were also used in fishing from small rafts. Great drives were organized for wild animals. As many as fifty or sixty thousand men were used to round up the game which was killed with stones and clubs or snared with the *bolas*, a clever primitive lasso, consisting of a rope with a heavy stone at each end, that was thrown and wound itself around the body or legs of the animal. The Saca Inca himself often accompanied these hunts. A large part of the catch were wild llamas, most of which were sheared and then turned loose.

An Inca portrait in pottery

THE ARTS

In science and learning Peru was far below the other classic cultures of America. As contrasted to the high development of astronomy by the Maya and the Aztecs, the Incas had only the crudest concepts of the relation of the earth to the other heavenly bodies. They had no flexible and efficient number system such as the Maya had so brilliantly worked out. They had no writing, not even picturegraphs. They did, however, use a clever device for keeping accounts and making reports. This was a series of knotted strings of various colors called *quipu*. Knots tied at specified places on the different strings, in accordance with a decimal system, recorded numbers running to high figures and classified under separate headings. Special scholars, called *quipucamayus* (keepers of the knots), used these strings in keeping accounts of births and deaths and marriages throughout the realm, in reporting the materials

Pottery was often moulded in the shape of animals

furnished by the state to artisans and the fabrics made from them, in recording the amount of stores of various kinds in the great warehouses of the several provinces. Collections of these *quipus* kept in Cuzco formed the national archives.

The Incas were a practical people. They were interested in the application of knowledge rather than in abstract learning. Less successful in exploring the heavens, they surpassed all other native Americans in dominating the earth. A royal epigram was 'He who attempts to count the stars and does not know how to count the marks and knots of the *quipus* ought to be held in derision.'

The making of pottery and textiles were great industries as well as fine arts. In early times the people moulded pots of graceful proportions with beautiful and intricate designs. Realistic pictures on old vases of historical scenes, religious festivals, and daily activities of the people are a rich source of

Designs on Inca textiles

information on life and customs in Peru. Many of the pots were moulded into the shapes of animals and men, some of them being portraits or cartoons of living persons. With the large-scale production demanded by the efficient Inca rulers there was loss of individuality in all the arts and crafts, and the later pottery became standardized into uniform shapes and geometric designs.

Textiles excelled anything known elsewhere in native America and are even today among the world's finest examples of weaving. The Incas had the great advantage over other Indians of having wool as a fiber. They also had two fine types of cotton, one pure white and the other a golden brown. And they used dyes with great skill: bright red from the little cochineal bugs and a wide variety of vegetable and mineral colorings.

Since spinning was all done by hand, a great deal of women's time had to be devoted to this task to furnish the thread and yarn used in the great textile industry of the Empire. Women

Beaten gold plaque

carried cotton or wool with them wherever they went. Even as they walked along the city streets or country roads or visited their neighbors, their fingers were busy making strands and winding them on spindles. When a woman went to call upon a person of higher rank she left her own work at home and immediately on arriving said humbly that she had not come to call but to see if she could help in some household task. A gracious hostess replied that she would not think of letting the guest do servant's work but that she would be glad to get some of the spinning or embroidery on which her daughters had been working. This was a compliment since it admitted the guest to the work and therefore to the social sphere of the high-born lady of the house.

The Peruvians also carried metal work far beyond the practices of other native Americans. Gold and silver, platinum and copper, were extensively used for both utensils and ornaments. In the working of metals the Incas were masters of the most intricate processes: smelting, the casting of molten ore in moulds, soldering and welding, and the hammering of metal into thin sheets and fine strands. Copper was the metal most widely used and, much more extensively than elsewhere among Indians, it served for tools as well as for ornaments, for knives and hammers and chisels as well as for bracelets and pendants. Much of the copper mined in Peru was mixed with tin and thus formed a natural bronze tougher and more durable than pure copper.

Gold was collected chiefly from deposits in the beds of rivers. But silver and other metals had to be dug out by regular mining. The work was hard and, in recognition of their arduous and important service, miners worked for but a few months each year and were exempt from all other labor. It is reported that the marriages of miners were supervised by high officials so that these prized servants of the state would be sure to have qualified persons to prepare their food and keep their homes.

The wealth in gold and silver and precious stones went chiefly into the glorification of the gods and the monarchs. The word for gold in the figurative Quichua language meant literally 'tears wept by the Sun,' and gold was constantly associated with the Sun and his delegates on earth. The Sun temple at Cuzco was studded with gold and gleaming gems. A great golden sunburst — as an image of the god — shone from the center of the altar wall and even on the outside of the temple a great frieze of gold circled the whole building. The Saca Inca had gardens in which stood images in gold and silver of all the trees and flowers of the region. These treasure grounds must have looked like the gardens of Midas where everything he touched turned to gold.

The Inca court represented a display of extravagant riches equal to that of any Oriental monarch. The Saca Inca sat on a throne of solid gold which rested on a golden platform. All of the utensils of the royal household were of gold or silver.

Small llama made of gold   *Thin gold cup*

When traveling the Inca was carried in a litter of the finest wood, studded with gold and jewels. In addition to the central palace at Cuzco, there were magnificent residences in the several suburbs and in all the principal cities of the Empire. It is recorded that for one of these palaces ten planks of solid silver each a foot wide and twenty feet long were used as decoration, and that for another palace a cement of gold was laid between the stones which formed the walls. Harems of beautiful girls were kept in all the chief centers for the entertainment of the monarch on his tours about the kingdom.

ENGINEERING

Engineering was the art in which the Incas produced their most spectacular feats. The Empire was held together by a great system of highways and branch roads. Two great Incaways stretched the whole length of the realm from Quito in the north to Tucuman, twenty-two hundred miles to the south. One road followed the coast line, the other the lofty region

The Empire was held together by a great system of highways

along the plateaus and highlands. These were connected by a
network of crossroads so that there was ready access to every
part of the Empire.

In describing the highways, Cieza de Leon, an early Spanish
traveler, says, 'Some of them extended over 1100 leagues along
such dizzy and frightful abysses that looking down the sight
failed. In some places to secure the regular width it was
necessary to hew a path out of the living rock; all of which was
done with fire and stone picks. In other places the ascents were
so steep and high that steps had to be cut from below to enable
the ascent to be made, with wider spaces at intervals for resting
places. Where the snows obstructed the way and where there
were forests and trees and loose clods of earth, the road was
paved with stones and leveled where necessary.' Since there
were no wheeled vehicles and travel was all by foot or pack
animal, the ways were narrow and, in climbing mountains,

*Rivers were crossed by swinging bridges, precipices scaled
by stairs cut in solid rock*

steps rather than roads were used. Passages were cut through
mountains, rivers were crossed by swinging bridges, ravines
were filled up with stone and earth, and precipices scaled by
galleries cut in the solid rock.

In the lowlands road building was not so difficult and the
great Inca-way along the coast was broad, paved with stone
slabs, protected by walls and shaded by trees. But in the desert
regions of the coast the shifting sand dunes made paving a
waste of time. Here the route was simply marked by tall poles
set in the earth at short distances.

Suspension bridges across rivers were spectacular features of
the highways. Five huge cables of woven willow rods were
stretched from bank to bank and made fast at either end to
rock or to masses of masonry erected for the purpose. Three of
the cables, each as large as a man's body and wrapped together
and protected from wear by layers of rushes, served as the floor

of the bridge while the other two strands served as hand rails and were connected with the floor cables by interlaced boughs. Such bridges, exceedingly strong, served for the passage of man and beast. Stone slabs twenty feet or more in length were used to bridge the smaller streams. Often, where the river current was not too strong, floating bridges made of bundles of reeds were used.

Along this system of roads relay runners conveyed messages with great dispatch. At intervals of about two miles there were small relay houses with two Indians, fully provisioned from the state stores, on guard. When an order was given or an event of note occurred, a man set out at great speed to the nearest of these houses, from which a runner would dash to the next relay point, and so on until messages were carried swiftly for hundreds of miles to the farthest limits of the Empire. It is reported that the relay runners carried messages from Cuzco to Quito, a distance of over one thousand miles as the crow flies and much farther by road, in less than eight days. One chronicle mentions a record of five days for this trip. These runners carried freight as well as messages, rushing fruit and fish and game from distant provinces to be served fresh on the royal table. In the case of an emergency such as an insurrection, when it would be impossible for a runner to spread news swiftly enough, a system of telegraph was used. Fires flashing smoke by day and flame by night were relayed along the post houses so that the report of an uprising a thousand miles away could reach Cuzco in two or three hours.

The Incas carried their engineering skill into their aqueducts and buildings. Though the principle of the true arch and keystone was unknown in native America, they built magnificent temples and palaces. They used bricks made of tough clay mixed with reeds and grass which withstood storms and

Fortress at the northern entrance of Cuzco

the fierce tropical sun, simply growing firmer with the centuries. They quarried and transported huge blocks of rock and invented a system of cutting their great building stones into shapes which could be keyed together, thus binding the masonry. The great Temple to the Sun at Cuzco is one of the striking monuments of the world. The stupendous fortress which guarded the northern entrance to the Capital is an equally impressive monument with individual stones thirty-eight feet long and running in total size to four thousand cubic feet. It is reported that this mighty fortress took the labor of twenty thousand men and was fifty years in building. In all this national labor the people were drafted whether they liked it or not. The heavy work on the great buildings took toll of thousands of lives. The Inca public works, like similar monuments the world over, are more than memorials to planning and art. They are the tombs of countless laborers.

RELIGION

The official religion of the Incas was the worship of the Sun. Conquests were partly religious crusades carried on for the purpose of forcing all people to accept the Sun god as the ruling deity. As each new province was conquered, the Inca at once built in it a temple to the Sun and carried back images of the local gods as captives. These images, interestingly enough, were not destroyed but were set up as subject deities in the great Sun temple at Cuzco. But so long as they acknowledged the Sun as the chief god, the people of the various provinces were allowed to continue their own religious practices very much as they pleased.

The faith of the masses had little to do with formal religion of any sort. Their fears and worship clustered about a great multitude of sacred objects called *huaca*. Rocks, lakes, animals, mummies of ancestors, sticks, stones and stars — all these were *huaca* to the people. Even the sun was in the popular mind simply the greatest of a host of holy objects. The concern of the people was mainly in gaining the favor or warding off the evil of the numerous *huaca*.

Religion in the minds of the Incas, as with many people, was especially associated with death. A great deal of attention was given to providing for the welfare of friends and relatives in the spirit world after death and to avoiding any evil which ghosts might do to the living. Bodies buried in the dry caves of the highlands or in the sand of the coastal deserts dried promptly and were thus, by natural processes, turned into mummies. Often the blood and entrails were removed from the bodies at death so that the mummifying process would be swifter and more complete. These mummies, especially the bodies of the Incas, were treated with reverence. They were worshipped as *huaca* by the common people and were given an honorable part in the ceremonies of the state religion. Wrapped in beautiful textiles and often surrounded by exquisite ornaments and vases, Inca mummies have been preserved through the ages and are to this day picturesque reminders of the glorious past of Peru.

In the more formal aspects of religion there were many ceremonies and festivals in worship of the Sun, the Moon, the Earth, and a whole series of lesser gods. The highest of the festivals was the great feast of the Sun, called *Intip Raymi*, held at the winter solstice, just as the sun was starting its annual return to greater heat and glory. This was an aristocratic ceremony: the worship of the Sun by his direct representatives on earth. To this feast nobles and officials came into Cuzco from all parts of the Empire, while all strangers and people of low degree were banished from the Capital. Nobles came pouring into the sacred city — from the mountains in robes of puma skin, from the coastal regions in apparel of finely woven cloth, from the east and north in raiment made of the brilliant plumage of birds, certain of the chiefs wearing condor costumes with magnificent outstretched wings.

A three-day fast preceded the main ceremony. Then just before sunrise on the great day, the gorgeously costumed company made up of the Saca Inca, Inca nobles, and officials of the state and church, assembled at the holy terrace or great square before the Temple of the Sun. All prostrated themselves, resting on their elbows with hands spread open on the ground and faces lifted up to receive the benediction of the first rays of the rising sun. As the sun streamed down upon the worshippers, the Saca Inca rose and lifting two vases filled with wine emptied one into a golden trough which carried the wine to the altar within the temple and passed the other among the high priests and nobles. Thus God and his worshippers drank together in holy communion.

Saca Inca and nobles worshipping the Sun at the festival Intip Raymi

New fire was made to usher in the new season. The high
priest started the sacred flame by concentrating the rays of the
sun from a concave mirror onto a wisp of cotton. If the day
were cloudy, the fire had to be made by the customary rubbing
together of two sticks, but when this happened it was an evil
omen for the coming year.

After burnt sacrifices of beasts and birds, the flesh was eaten
as a sacrament, together with little cakes specially prepared by
the temple virgins. Then followed riotous feasting for nine
days. The drinking started with great ceremony in accordance
with a regular etiquette. A man of higher degree would honor
his neighbors of lower state by drinking with them in turn, and
the men so honored were supposed to return the courtesy. For
nine days and nine nights the feast went on. As the hours
passed, pomp turned into riot, the ceremony into an orgy.
Drinking became an endurance contest and many fell in the
course of it.

Another festival, in honor of the Moon (*Coya Raymi*, wife of
the Sun), was held toward the beginning of the rainy season in
September and was an official cleansing and blessing of the
city of Cuzco. Sacred objects from all over the Empire were
brought to the Capital and all strangers, all the sick, and all
persons known to be unlucky were driven out of the city for
the days of the ceremony. At the rising of the moon on the
night of the festival, four groups of armed men, one hundred in
each band, started in the four directions from the city square,
brandishing weapons and shouting, 'Go forth all Evils.' As
these warriors reached the countryside they put off their armour
and plunged into the near-by rivers, praying their ills to flow
away with the running waters or to glide from the earth along
the silvery rays of the moon. Meanwhile all citizens came out
of their houses, shook their mantles, crying, 'Let the Evils be

gone,' and purified themselves for the coming year by bathing
in the streams under the light of the moon. Next day the
images and other sacred objects, including important mummies,
were brought out into the square and washed. The festival
ended with feasting and dancing and the sacrifice of many
llamas.

Another holiday was devoted to weddings. On one day
each year all the boys and girls who had reached marriageable
age — about twenty years for men, and eighteen for girls —
were brought into the public squares of the cities and villages
to be married. If the young people or their parents had not
selected mates, the officials arbitrarily paired them off. Thus
weddings, and in due course the production of children, were
tended by the busy bureaucracy of this efficient Empire.

Many maidens were raised in convents for service to the
temples and the gods. A number of convent girls, selected for
'the beauty of their bodies and their dispositions,' entered the
harems of the Saca Inca and the Inca nobles. But for the most
part they were trained to devote their lives to temple service.
In the convents the girls slept in small stone cells, watched over
and instructed by a Mother Superior and a corps of spinsters.
These girls spun and wove all the ceremonial garments for
the Saca Inca and for the priests and nobles, and made all the
wine and holy bread used in offerings to the gods and in the
sacred feasts. There is evidence that these sacred virgins were
sometimes used for human sacrifices, though the Incas did
much to wipe out this practice which was common among
many of the native peoples before they became parts of the
Empire.

Knighthood very similar to the chivalry of medieval Europe
flourished among the young nobles. During the years just
preceding manhood, sons of the Inca nobility and of the

highest officials served a novitiate which combined religious and patriotic instruction with schooling in hardihood and warfare. Each year a strange kind of graduation service was held for all these noble scholars who had reached the age of sixteen. They presented themselves for a nine-day ordeal called *Huaracu* (the putting on of the loincloth) which was at once an initiation ceremony and an elimination contest. After a six-day fast, they ran a foot race of more than five miles, followed this with athletic contests, and then for two successive days held a sham battle in which half the candidates stormed a fortress while the other half defended it. In the course of the ordeal they were flogged to prove their fortitude, set on long vigils of sentry duty, and subjected to attack by skilled warriors brandishing clubs and spears. The slightest sign of faltering or flinching in any of the trials brought disgrace.

Those novices who succeeded in all the tests were admitted to knighthood in an impressive ceremony. The Saca Inca, surrounded by the highest princes of the blood, received the homage of each candidate and then with royal hands pierced the ears with a golden bodkin and inserted the badge of honor, the special ear bobs which were worn only by nobles and knights. Other high Inca nobles took each youth to a special apartment and placed about his loins the *huara* (loincloth) which gave the name to the ceremony. Adorned with the ear bobs and the *huara*, the youth stood forth a man and a knight.

CLASH OF EMPIRE

The greatest of Inca arts was government. No nation either in ancient or modern times has succeeded so efficiently in the economic planning of a whole great realm. This meant regimentation, an absence of personal freedom and individual initiative that to North American Indians and to most modern people would seem intolerable, though the docile Peruvians seemed to take it as a matter of course. Art, engineering, farming, crafts, all were devoted under a thoroughly planned economy to the well-being of the entire nation. Almost universal peace was guaranteed by the strength of the Empire. Pride and satisfaction came through exercise of individual skill and through sharing in the glories of the realm. Amid free expression in various religious cults, there was spiritual unity in the universal worship of the Sun and in adoration of the Sun's personal deputy on earth, the majestic ruler of the Empire, the Saca Inca.

It was because of a break in the godhood of rule that the Spaniards under Pizarro in 1531 were able to take the Empire so easily. Fate seemed to be against the Indians at every crucial point in the European invasion. When Pizarro and his little army came adventuring into Peru, a pretender named Atahualpa had seized the Inca throne. Huayna, the last great Inca, had become very fond of Atahualpa, his son by a secondary wife, a Quito princess. The sacred law of the realm (similar to the rule for the Pharaohs in ancient Egypt) was that the Saca Inca could have as his official wife only his own sister and that inheritance to the throne could come only to a son born to that sister-wife. Thus the new emperor would be of pure stock, a 'child of the Sun,' by both his parents. On his deathbed Huayna tried to break this law and ordered that his true heir by his sister-wife should reign only over the southern kingdom and that Atahualpa, who was only half an Inca, should rule Quito and the northern realm. This not only divided the Empire, but destroyed a great part of the authority and holiness of the monarchy. Civil war broke out, during which the strong army of Quito highlanders led by Atahualpa took the true Inca prisoner.

In the midst of this confusion the Spaniards came. Pizarro, by a series of treacheries, seized Atahualpa when he had come unarmed on a friendly visit, slyly brought about the murder of the true Inca in his prison, and then had Atahualpa strangled. Immediately the whole machinery of Inca government was paralyzed. Without a dictator the bureaucracy was helpless, the army unable to move. And the people, untrained in initiative, had no means of defending themselves. Years of following orders had made puppets of them and with the capture of the Inca who had for so long pulled the strings, the Peruvians were as helpless as marionettes without a master. It was as if a clock had been stopped simply by seizing the mainspring, although all the rest of the machinery remained in order. Controlling this mainspring, Pizarro and his Spanish army controlled the whole huge Empire.

The little band of adventurers who made up Pizarro's army desired only gold and power. While some of the priests and colonists who came later were unselfish, most of the Spaniards who poured in from 'civilized' Europe were driven by greed. They cared nothing for the high arts and efficient economy which the Incas had built up. They let the highways fall into decay; even the poles set up to mark the coastal roads over the sand dunes were torn up and burned as firewood. They destroyed the flocks of tame llamas and began hunting so wantonly that the wild animals and game which had been carefully preserved under the Incas were almost wiped out. They let the irrigation system fall into decay and soon the prosperous coastal regions reverted to desert. They tore up graves, looted temples, melted the most exquisitely wrought ornaments, and enslaved a whole population in their mad scramble for gold. They disrupted the orderly farming and looted the great storehouses of grain, and soon want and hunger spread over the country. They trampled on the religion and traditions of the people and shattered the life of a whole great nation.

The Incas had built up a high civilization. In the clumsy hands of the conquerors the delicate machinery of government was wrecked, the carefully balanced economy fell apart, the arts died.

ESKIMO

AREA

NORTH PACIFIC
COAST AREA

MACKENZIE AREA

PLATEAU

EASTERN WOODLAND AREA

CALIFORNIA

AREA

PLAINS AREA

SOUTHEASTERN AREA

AREA

SOUTHWESTERN AREA

*Map of North
American culture areas
with typical house used in each region*

HG

NORTH AMERICAN
INDIAN LIFE

WHILE ART AND LEARNING were flourishing in Central America
and Mexico and Peru, many other types of life developed
throughout the continent. In North America above the Rio
Grande (the region which is now the United States and
Canada) there was an almost limitless diversity of societies and
modes of life. None of these North American Indians achieved
the heights of art and learning of the classic cultures, but they
led colorful lives, full of zest and joy to themselves, full of
interest to the student of mankind.

It is hard to classify the various North American Indians
into groups that have much meaning. Settling and moving
about on this great continent for thousands of years, Indian
groups separated and lived by themselves for long periods,
then in the course of further migrations mingled, and in turn
separated again. So in their blood and their customs were
many mixtures. Scholars have tried to group them by the
languages they spoke, the way they lived, and their appearance.
These groupings naturally overlap one another and in each

one there are almost as many diversities as similarities. But a few rough classifications can be made.

The North American Indians fall into about a dozen major language stocks, plus a great many smaller units whose tongues are so distinct as to require separate classification. Members of the several groups do not speak one language but tongues sufficiently related as to seem to come from a common root. In the same way in modern Europe we speak of the Latin language group, including French, Spanish, and Italian, or the Slavic stock — Russian, Czech, Serbian, etc. So the various Indian peoples are grouped into related language stocks, though the several tribes within the groups may speak such variants of the language as often to be unintelligible to one another.

The main linguistic divisions in native North America, as shown on the map on page 117, are made up for the most part of tribes which had long lived near one another. But they also include people living at great distances from the main areas and following very different customs from the main groups.

The Algonquian language stock included not only the Algonkin Indians of the St. Lawrence Valley but also the Abnaki confederation of northern New England, many tribes of the Midwest and Great Lakes region — Illinois, Kickapoo, Potawotami, etc. — certain of the tribes of the Great Plains — Blackfoot, Cheyenne, Arapaho — and even people as far west as California. There is a common root to the speech of the five nations which made up the Iroquois League, their early neighbors — the Huron and Erie — and even people who were as far from them as the Cherokee of the South. The great language group called Athapascan, composed chiefly of people of the far North, also includes the Navajo and Apache of the Southwest. The Shoshonean stock covers not only the

Map of North American language groups

Shoshone Indians and their neighbors in the Rocky Mountains and southern plateaus but also the Hopi group of the Pueblo Indians and a number of tribes in southern California and Mexico. The Siouan language group includes the Sioux and many of their neighbors on the Great Plains, a number of tribes of the midwest prairies — Iowa, Omaha, Osage — and people who once lived as far east as Virginia and the Carolinas on the Atlantic seaboard and as far south as Mississippi on the Gulf of Mexico.

Scholars have also classified the various Indian peoples by the modes of life of the different regions. These 'culture areas,' shown on the map on page 114, are rough divisions, for many variations are found within each region.

Customs or cultures seem to have been influenced more by the territory in which the people lived than by blood relationship. Yet even the same environment did not always produce similar types of culture. It is true that in most cases the tribes which lived fairly close together had much in common. Those on the Great Plains, for example, although they were of different stocks and languages, built similar ways of life to fit the wide expanse of the prairies and the pursuit of the buffalo. Most of the various groups living in the eastern woodlands in and about the present New York State combined hunting and fishing and farming, built warm bark and log houses against the hard winters, and developed almost identical customs. But, also in the woodlands, there were nomadic people who knew no agriculture and lived mainly on the seeds they gathered. The various village dwellers of the Southwest — the Zuñi and Hopi and those living along the Rio Grande — who spoke different tongues and probably came from different stocks, had similar customs built around farming and village life. Yet their near neighbors, the Navajo and Apache, were roving hunters directly opposite in their mode of life to the settled farmers of the villages.

Classifications are also made on the basis of bodily structure and appearance. While all Indians have in general the features of their Mongoloid ancestors — yellow or brown skin, straight, coarse black hair, and high cheek bones — there are many minor differences between tribes. The Hopi and Comanche, for example, are short and swarthy. The Sioux and Navajo tend to have tall bodies and somewhat lighter skin. Several of the Shoshone tribes have broad faces, while the Algonkins have long, narrow heads.

In addition to the major groups, there are a number of tribes so different from their fellow Indians in language and habits as to require special classifications even for groups as small as a few hundred families. A score or more of such distinct peoples lived on the Pacific Coast.

The varieties among the Indians are so great that it is clearly impossible to give any single outline of native life in North America. All that can be done is to give sample pictures. Any number of samples might be chosen.

There is the fascinating story of the wild, colorful Navajo of the Southwest whose raids brought constant terror to their settled neighbors. Swooping down upon the peaceful Pueblo villagers, they carried away corn and vegetables and cotton, women and children. From their captives the Navajo learned so well the art of weaving by loom that today they are famous the world over for their blankets. Beyond other North American Indians, they were the poets, the musicians, the artists. Deeply religious, they gave expression to their faith in numberless legends, in thousands of songs and prayers, in elaborate and finely-wrought sand paintings, in endless dances and ceremonies. Although highly courageous in war and the hunt, they so feared the dead that no Navajo dared enter a house in which a person had died. This feeling is so strong to this day that Navajo villages are dotted with deserted hogans. Even a dream of the dead is frightening enough to call for the services of a medicine man and purification ceremonies.

There are the Cherokee, that stalwart race of mountaineers who lived in the Alleghenies and surrounding lands of the Southeast. These people built a life of simple farming and a society organized on the basis of brotherhoods or 'towns' which, in spite of migrations and persecutions, continue to this day. One of the saddest chapters in early American history was the forced removal of the Cherokee from the lands of their ancestors, an uprooting which brought illness and heartbreak to a whole people and death to four thousand in the course of their terrible march westward. To the south of the Cherokee lived four other great tribes: the tall and graceful Creeks, devoted equally to music, ball games and war, with their strong confederation of towns in Alabama and Georgia — red towns of war and white towns of peace — who became the prosperous owners of many Negro slaves; the Seminoles who split off from their brother Creeks and made their home in Florida; the Choctaw, most successful farmers of all the southern Indians, who never fought unless they were forced to defend themselves; the brave and warlike Chickasaw, with their great towns along the lower Mississippi Valley, who warred constantly with neighboring tribes — even with their close relatives, the Choctaw. These groups, transplanted to adjoining lands in the Indian Territory, are today known as the Five Civilized Tribes because of the success with which they have copied white methods of living.

It would be interesting to write of the Pawnee in their earth lodges along the Platte River, with their scalp locks stiffened by

Map showing location, at time of white contact, of North American Indians mentioned in this book

fat and paint to stand up on their heads like curved horns. Even more than most Plains Indians, they were devoted to their sacred bundles, and in every lodge this precious gift from the Great Spirit hung in the place of honor to guarantee protection and guidance, while in important religious ceremonies the bundles were publicly opened and worshipped. Hated by other Indian tribes, the Pawnee were without a single friend on the vast prairies. Their enemies included the Dakota and Crow on the north, the Ute, Arapaho, and Cheyenne on the west, the Comanche, Kansas, Osage, Kiowa, and even their close kin, the Wichita, on the south. They became known as 'wolves' probably from their custom of disguising themselves in wolf skins when on the warpath. Certainly they had the endurance of wolves for they could travel by foot, burdened by heavy loads, six and eight hundred miles. It was their habit to sneak up and kill sleeping enemies or to shoot from behind, for it was not considered good form to take needless risks. The prestige of a war leader depended more on returning with all men unharmed than on the number of enemies slain. Because of their unceasing hostility, the Pawnee were constantly being attacked. Even before the coming of the white man, bringing death with his whiskey and diseases, the Pawnee wars had taken great toll of the population.

Of peculiar interest would be the story of the Kwakiutl of British Columbia whose way of life, unlike that of most Indians, was based on a system of credit and interest with a money economy of huge copper sheets each valued at ten thousand blankets or more. The most valued possessions of this capitalistic group were nobility titles which demanded the distribution of great wealth at potlatch ceremonies given on every important occasion in life. But those who received the gifts had to return their equivalent, with excessive interest, on pain of permanent disgrace. The surest form of revenge, therefore, was to make a gift so valuable that an enemy could not return it. Accidents and even death were thought of as affronts so shameful that expensive gifts had to be made to pay for the humiliation. The Kwakiutl, and their neighbors, the Nootka, who had a similar money economy, were distinguished also by their habit of hunting whale in their log canoes and their fashion of flattening the skull by binding boards to the soft heads of babies.

Other people of the Pacific slope are equally interesting: the Haida, the best carvers and canoe builders of all the people of the northwest coast, with their great totem poles, their habit of tattooing on their hands and arms the family name and connection, their belief in reincarnation; and the primitive tribes of California who lived almost entirely on acorns and wild seeds and used only crude rafts on the water.

It would be instructive to follow the Mohegans who, with their neighbors the Pequots and Wampanoags and other Algonquian tribes, were in New England when the Pilgrims landed, and whose resourcefulness in woodcraft and war (celebrated in the Leatherstocking Tales of James Fenimore Cooper) have thrilled American boys for generations. There is similar attraction to the stories of the groups who met the other colonists: the Virginia Indians led by the friendly chief, Powhatan, father of the romantic Pocahontas; the Delawares of Pennsylvania with their intricate social organization by clans and tribes and council fires, their honorable dealings with William Penn and his Society of Friends, and their wars with the Iroquois.

There were equally fascinating tribes in the Midwest: the Sauk and Fox, 'the people of the yellow earth' and 'the people of the red earth,' fierce hunters of the woodlands around the Great Lakes; the Shawnee, who roamed from the Savannah River on the eastern seaboard to the upper stretches of the Ohio; the Ottawa, from early times so interested in barter of cornmeal and furs and tobacco among the neighboring tribes that they were given their name, which means 'traders,' and who in warm weather went about stark naked, decorating their bodies only with intricate tattooing; the Chippewa, called 'pointed skins' because they wore shirts pointed and ornamented with tails, who ate the wild rice found around Lake Superior and who, with their relatives, the Ottawa, fashioned the finest birchbark canoes in native America.

Scores of other diverse people throughout the continent would be equally worthy of study. From the wealth of North American native life, pictures are given in this book of three groups: the Indians of the Great Plains, the Iroquois of the eastern woodlands, the Pueblos of the Southwest.

The Indians of the Plains

LIFE ON THE
WESTERN PLAINS

A COLORFUL LIFE grew up in the vast inland plains of North America between the Mississippi River and the Rocky Mountains. Here Indians roamed in small bands, setting up temporary camps and moving them frequently as the seasons changed and as the herds of buffalo shifted from one grazing ground to another. The great open spaces, the pursuit of game, and the dependence upon wild nature made the life rugged and daring.

Existence on the western plains was built around two animals: the buffalo and the horse. The buffalo, whose meat and hides and bones were sufficient to supply almost all the needs of primitive man, were native to America, had probably been lazily wandering over the prairies for thousands of years before the first ancestors of the Indians came over to this world from Asia. But horses were new. Unknown in native America, they were brought in from Europe by the early Spanish adventurers. Some of the Spanish horses wandered northward, running wild; others were traded or stolen from tribe to tribe. As early as 1540 horses began to appear in the southwestern villages and by 1760 they were common throughout much of the region from the Mississippi to the Rockies.

Indians, especially in the central regions of North America, hailed these new animals with joy and quickly rebuilt their lives to the scope and dash which horses made possible. Probably no people have ever taken up a new toy or a new tool more rapidly or more effectively than the Plains Indians adopted the horse. For more than a hundred years Indians of the Plains used these horses, introduced to the continent by the white man, before they came into any serious contact with the white man himself.

Before the coming of the horse there had been life on the Plains. But it had been cramped and limited. Only small populations could exist, moving their camps on foot, with dogs dragging the baggage on wooden poles, as they followed the wandering herds of buffalo over the great arid spaces. It is true that many Indian tribes had lived on the fringes of the Plains: in what is now Illinois and Wisconsin and Minnesota on the east, northern New Mexico and Texas on the south, the Great Basin area and Canada on the west and north. With their home base in these more fertile regions, many Indians made temporary encampments on the Plains, but depended for their food more on the game and crops around their settled homes than on the buffalo of the bare prairies. But when the horse appeared (making it possible to cover the vast distances of the open plains, to follow the buffalo herds, to travel scores of miles in search of water and fresh vegetation), Indians from many surrounding areas moved into the Plains and made their homes there.

The people that we speak of as Plains Indians were thus made up of many diverse groups who moved in from widely separated regions and were descended from differing stocks. Thirty-one separate groups or peoples are classified by scholars as making up the Plains Indians, of which the most typical are the Teton-

With dogs dragging the baggage on wooden poles

Dakota (Sioux), Blackfoot, Crow, and Gros Ventre, on the northern plains, and the Arapaho, Cheyenne, Comanche, and Kiowa in the southern part of the region. But these tribes spoke such different languages and had such other variations that they must have come from widely separated peoples. The Comanche, for example — short, dark men — spoke a Shoshone tongue related to the Aztecs of Mexico and the Hopi branch of the Pueblos. The Crow and the Teton-Dakota — tall, fine-bodied people — were members of the Siouan language group. The Arapaho, Blackfoot, and Cheyenne spoke Algonquian dialects related to the speech of such distant people as the Mohegans and Delawares and other tribes of New England and the eastern seaboard.

Since these various tribes, living in the same general region, spoke different languages, they learned to talk by signs made with their hands and bodies. In this sign language an idea could be expressed so simply that it was easily understood, and this means of communication spread until it was recognized as the universal language of the Plains. A Sioux Indian, for example, on meeting a Blackfoot, could tell him that he was tired and hungry simply by moving his two hands downward and outward in front of his body (fatigue) and then drawing his hand horizontally across his stomach (hunger). Or he might tell the stranger that he had left home two nights before by making the sign for tipi (bringing both index fingers together to form a triangle), holding up two fingers, and leaning his head to one side above his open palm to indicate sleep or night.

The peoples living in the prairie country not only spoke different languages and differed from one another in appearance, but had forms of ceremonies and social organization which, while similar in outline, had definite tribal distinctions. When therefore we speak of Plains Indians we are using a very general term to describe the many different peoples who built their life around the buffalo, the horse, the camp circle, and special customs adapted to this grand, wild, open country.

A good deal is known of the daily life of various groups of Plains Indians during their great era which extended from the time horses came into use until the white men crowded into the western country. From stories passed down by both Indians and white pioneers and from remnants of the old customs that still exist we can picture pretty accurately the life of a hundred and fifty years ago. And perhaps the most vivid way of giving the general picture is to follow the adventures and daily actions of a family within a specific tribe.

LIFE AMONG THE OGLALA SIOUX

On the plains of the rolling Dakotas lay a circle of tipis, the encampment of several bands of the Oglala division of the Teton-Dakota tribe of Sioux Indians. In the center of the great circle stood the council tent, occupied now by the chiefs and elders of the several bands. They sat cross-legged on the ground, smoking their long pipes as they talked. Among them was

Standing Buffalo in front of his tipi

Standing Buffalo, chief of the Red Cloud Band. He was a tall, powerfully built man, and though fifty winters had passed over him the long hair which hung to his waist was as black as it had ever been. The strong, bronze body, covered only by a loin-cloth, showed many scars, relics of the tortures he had willingly borne in the religious ceremonies, and the little finger of his left hand was gone, for this he had cut off many years before in sacrifice to the Wakan Tanka, the sacred spirit.

Standing Buffalo was now a man of distinction. He had become a chief through the regular steps of promotion from moccasin bearer to water carrier to scout. He had honored himself by stealing many horses from enemy bands. Always he was in the front in battle. He had often counted first coup by being foremost in touching the bodies of his foes, and he had counted other coups — second, third, fourth — by being among those first four daring warriors to touch the enemy. He had been wounded twice, saved the life of a friend, led many war parties, and had ten scalps of enemy Crows hanging in his tipi. He was known to be generous, offering feasts for his friends and giving away many horses and robes to the poor. On his tipi were painted signs for all of his deeds and the picture of a great pot boiling over a fire to show that here was a place where any who were hungry might come and be fed. Standing Buffalo was more than an ordinary chief. He was one of the directing powers of the band, for years ago he had been made a shirt-wearer, an office he would hold for life, and now he and three other shirt-wearers were responsible for the welfare of the group. He had but a short time before taken a second woman and, according to Sioux custom, had chosen the younger sister of his first wife so that there would be no quarreling in his tipi. Because of his prowess his two wives were members of the shield bearers' society and his sons bore honored names: Kills Many Enemies and Steals Horses.

A BUFFALO HUNT

For a calm, summer evening the camp was unusually quiet — no singing and dancing and storytelling. Interest was centered on the tipi where the chiefs and elders sat in council, for food had run low and even the children knew that a buffalo hunt was being planned. The people sat chatting of unimportant things but their eyes were on the council tent in the center of the great circle. Abruptly the chattering voices stopped as, at a sign from the council, the camp crier rode around the circle naming the four who had been selected to scout for buffalo. Almost at once these young men appeared at the council tent with their bows and arrows and wearing only loincloth and moccasins. The glow of the fire lit up the eager, bronze faces, and men and women sang in encouragement and praise as the scouts, led by Good Runner, sped four times around the flames then dashed off into the darkness.

Through the night the camp was quiet but restless with the expectancy of the great hunt to come. When the morning sky began to lighten in the east, the crier made the rounds of the tipis calling out that it was time to get ready. The council tent came down and, at this signal, the Indians prepared to break camp. Women bustled about their packing.

Just as the sun showed its face, the camp crier shouted the news. The scouts were coming! By the time they reached the camp, a pile of buffalo chips had been prepared, and men, women, and children were standing behind it, watching anxiously to see what the scout leader would do. Good Runner sped swiftly toward the pile of buffalo chips and kicked at it, scattering them in the four directions. A great shout rang out. The news was good! The people stood silently by as one of the old men lit a large pipe, puffed at it and, bending reverently to the earth, touched the ground with the bowl of the pipe as he held

the stem upward toward the sky. Then he handed the pipe to
Good Runner and spoke:

'You are no longer a child. You have grown up among these
hills and valleys. Tell me, have you seen anything — a prowling
wolf or feeding buffalo — beyond the hills from whence you
came? Tell me the facts and make my heart glad.'

Good Runner took the pipe, pointed it to heaven and earth,
puffed at it and passed it on to his three comrades. 'How' (yes)
he said simply, and 'Haye' (many thanks) the people chanted.

Urged once again by the old man, Good Runner told of the
great herd grazing near Big Water Creek beyond the Hill of
the Red Stones. Because the buffalo were resting quietly, he
was sure there were no enemies near. At the end of his report
all went away except the four wakichunsa (leaders of the camp
when it moved) and the head akichita (police) who stayed on to
arrange for the breaking of camp and the hunt. Six young men
were named to kill buffalo for the old and weak. The tokala
society, which had been chosen as police for the season, would
keep order while the camp traveled.

Quickly the children climbed to the top of the tipis to remove the sticks which held them together. One by one the tents came down and soon the poles and skins, together with buffalo robes, horn ladles and stone tools, were spread upon the ground in great confusion. Shaggy pack horses stood patiently while the tipi poles were lashed to their sides and masses of baggage tied upon the travois formed by these poles.

Everywhere there was the holiday spirit that always came with the moving of camp. The prospect of long days of roaming, a hunt, and plenty of food was more than enough to make the people happy. Boys boasted of the fleetness of their horses and raced ahead to prove their claims. Young braves, bright with paint and feathers, sat astride gayly ornamented ponies which kicked out at the dogs yapping at their heels. Naked children ran happily about. Smiling women gossiped as they led the heavy pack horses, while others rode, their babies cooing comfortably in the cradles tied to their mothers' backs.

Throughout the day the Indians moved slowly along over the rough prairie and the green hills, across streams, down into deep ravines and up again on level ground. For three days the bands traveled and four times each day the wakichunsa seated themselves on the ground and smoked, the fourth sitting being the signal to pitch camp for the night. When the Indians had come as close as they dared to the buffalo grounds, they set up their hunting camp while the hunters rode on, leading their best horses to keep them fresh for the chase.

As the riders reached the top of a hill they saw below them the great herd. But excited and eager as the men were, they waited for the order. None dared charge, for the akichita, armed with heavy war clubs, watched carefully, prepared to punish any who might shoot and stampede the herd before all were ready.

Now the buffalo had sensed their enemies, and young calves crowded close to the buffalo cows which were beginning to mill and bellow in restless confusion. When the hunters were all in position, the signal was given. Down to the valley the men rode, shooting arrow after arrow into the ranks of frightened, stampeding animals. Neither the hot sun beating down upon the Indians nor the clouds of choking, blinding dust which swept into their eyes and mouths halted them. For the smell of the beasts was like a stimulant to the excited men, and the thundering hoofs and frightened bellowing, the whizz of flying arrows which brought great bodies down, their own wild cries — all combined in a song of the plains, chanting of danger and bravery, sport and excitement, the promise of plenty and happiness.

Soon — all too soon for the hunters — the police signalled to stop shooting. Enough buffalo had been killed for the camp, and it was the fixed rule of the Indians never to slaughter more than could be used. In the distance the remnants of the herd could be seen running heavily away to safer grounds. The dust raised by flying hoofs slowly cleared away, and the dripping horses stood in panting exhaustion.

The herald brought out the old people so that they might take charge of the animals killed for them, and the women came to do their share of the skinning and butchering. The meat and hides were piled upon the horses for the journey back to the hunting camp, and with the return of the singing procession of triumphant hunters the whole camp began joyous preparations for the great feast.

IN CAMP

Next day the settlement was alive with chatter and activity. All over the camp meat hung from tall frames out of reach of the dogs and the wolves. After it had dried in the sun it would

*After hanging meat on a rack to dry, Standing Buffalo's two
wives clean a hide*

be stored for winter use. The women would be busy for days making pemmican of pounded buffalo meat and choke cherries. The bladder skins were bursting with marrow carefully scraped from inside the bones. Horns were waiting to be carved into spoons and ladles. There was plenty of sinew for thread and bowstrings, bones for war clubs and scrapers, hoofs for glue to fasten the arrow points, hair to be woven into belts and ornaments and ropes.

Steals Horses, the younger son of Standing Buffalo, with the freedom of a boy, wandered about the camp. He watched his two mothers at their work of preparing buffalo hides for use as covers and robes and tipis. On the ground near the tipi they stretched out a large skin which they pegged to the earth with wooden stakes. Bent almost double over the hide, they raked the flesh, scraping the skin down to an even thickness. The women in the next tipi were even further along. They were already rubbing oily fat and brains into the surface of the hide with firm, massaging strokes. When the whole skin had been covered with the fatty mess, they took a smooth stone, rubbing it slowly up and down until the fat was thoroughly worked in, and then hung it in the sun to dry.

While the women worked, their babies lay naked on the grass near-by. Here and there little girls played at being women, with their tiny buckskin tipis and puppies cradled on their backs like babies; and little boys raced, played follow-the-leader, and had mock buffalo hunts, or made a game of ferociously ripping grass scalps off wooden enemies with their toy tomahawks. One little chap of five summers played a captured foe and spat forth taunts as his tormentors held heated stones against his skin. The child laughed at his fierce captors, defying them to hurt him as he sang a Sioux death song.

In contrast to the sturdy child who would one day be a

warrior, Steals Horses saw a young man dressed as a girl deftly embroidering moccasins. Though the sight was strange, the lad did not laugh for he knew that a few men always lived as women — those who, in their vision quest, had seen a woman's sewing or cooking equipment.

Walking on about the camp, Steals Horses paused, here to look at a design on a rawhide bag taking shape under skilful fingers, there to watch an old brave make a pipestem of a stalk of young ash or a pipe bowl out of red stone. And everywhere he paid careful attention to what the men did for some day he too would learn to make pipes and rattles and war whistles, carve spoons and ladles, and prepare his own bows and arrows and war clubs.

As always after a hunt, the camp was gay with social affairs. Soldiers' societies and women's societies had their dances, and the camp crier was kept busy announcing the many feasts. Kills Many Enemies, the eldest son of Standing Buffalo, was allowed to join the men's entertainments. He liked to sit with the older men and listen to their stories. From them he heard how the Oglala crossed the Mud Water (Missouri River) the winter that Wearer of a Scarlet Robe was killed; how in their eastern home they had seen strange pale-faced men. It was from them that the Sioux first got the odd weapons which shot out little death-dealing pebbles. That was before the Oglalas saw the mysterious dogs (horses) which came to them in trade with the friendly Indians to the south.

Kills Many Enemies laughed as a favorite storyteller would get up and mimic the ugly white men with long hair on their faces who lived shut up in boxes and wore tight clothes which kept the sun from their bodies. The orator would wrap himself in robes from head to foot and, holding a tail from a dead horse under his chin, strut stiffly about, muttering queer sounds to imitate the white man's language, while his audience shouted with laughter.

Many jokes were made at the expense of the hobus (fops) who had elk visions and thus had great power over women. The old warriors grunted as they spoke of these men whose sole purpose was to win women counts rather than war counts. The hobus would spend much time brushing their long hair, adorning it with headbands of fur, and scenting themselves with the perfume of sweet-smelling seeds. Dressed in elaborately fringed and embroidered elkskin shirt and leggings, with long ornaments hanging from their ears, and armed with their powerful elk love medicine, the dandies made a game of conquering the women who pleased them.

There were tales of young men whom the police had punished for stealing from their friends by tearing their tipis to bits and depriving them of all their horses; of those who, in their vision quests, had seen and talked with frogs or night hawks and therefore had to become heyoka (clowns), acting like fools for the rest of their lives; of a man who had been a coward in war and, being shunned by the whole tribe, had sought death at the hands of an enemy brave; of attacks by the Crows and of war parties against them; of the dances and feasts of the tokala, ihoka, and other soldier societies; and of the Sun Dance, most important of the religious ceremonies.

A VISION QUEST

While Kills Many Enemies mingled with the older men, his young brother Steals Horses was busy with preparations for a vision quest. He was old enough now to commune with the great spirits above and seek from them guidance for his future life. The Wakan Tanka would send him a vision of the guardian spirit who would teach him to protect himself from his enemies

Preparing the sweat lodge for Steals Horses

and perhaps help him to become a leader of the tribe. Lest he make some slight mistake and thus antagonize the Wakan Tanka, Steals Horses scrupulously performed each task prescribed in the seeking of a vision.

He brought the horse his father had given him to Fast Whirlwind, a medicine man, offered him a pipe, and asked his guidance. For almost a moon Fast Whirlwind taught Steals Horses what he must know and do in order to seek a vision. The boy purified himself by prayer. He went to the sweat lodge where he crouched, sprinkling water on the heated stones pushed through the opening, until the little house was filled with steam, and then, naked, the sweat pouring from his body, he ran to a near-by stream to plunge into the cold water. At last, purified in mind and body, he was ready for his ordeal. When the setting sun was but a hand's breadth above the edge of the world, accompanied by the medicine man, Steals Horses set out for a distant hill. There the old man left him alone to fast and pray, promising to return each morning and evening.

Two days and two nights dragged by while Steals Horses, far away and alone, lying on a space he had cleared of every growing thing, prayed to the Wakan Tanka for a vision, his parched throat and empty stomach crying out for the food and water he could not touch. At the beginning of each prayer he pointed his pipe solemnly in the four directions.

'Wakan Tanka, onshimayala' (Great Mysterious, have pity on me), he prayed. 'I appreciate the Sun and the Moon and the Stars and the Blue Sky and the Thunder Trails and the Mountains and My Grandfather the Rocks and the Waters which give life and everything that stands upright. I thank you for these and for Mother Earth with all her creatures that crawl on the face of the world. Wakan Tanka, onshimayala.'

And on the third day Steals Horses returned, lean and haggard. His arms were covered with gashes from flesh offerings to the Sun, but he was singing a song of victory. In his vision he had seen and talked with a black-tailed deer. Since the boy did not understand the meaning of the vision, he went at once to a medicine man of the black-tailed deer cult who explained that now, like the deer, he would be able to scent any danger, that he must publicly perform a dance dressed as the deer, and that ever afterward he must carry sage, the deer's food, as protection from harm. The medicine man prepared a medicine bundle for him which the boy must never let out of his keeping.

Steals Horses felt he had been favored by the Great Mysterious, for though all men tried at some time in their lives many did not succeed in their vision quests. Now that he had power, he too, like his brother, would be strong in war. Or, if he wished, he might some day become a shaman (medicine man).

Steals Horses sought out his brother to talk about his future, but Kills Many Enemies was in no mood for talk. There were other, more important, matters on his mind. His courting was not going well. Through long nights he and other braves sat outside the tipi of Red Elk, but the girl did not come out. Instead her mother would appear to offer the courtesy of food to the waiting suitors. Kills Many Enemies could not even get a chance to speak to the girl to plead his cause, yet he was comforted by the thought that the other braves fared no better. He considered ways to advance his suit. He was a good hunter, had three horses, and had shown bravery in two war parties. But it was plain that this was not enough for Red Elk. Well then, he had power enough to lead his own war party. He would take his friends out on the warpath, bring home many horses and honor counts, and win the respect of the whole camp.

THE WAR PARTY

The young brave went at once to make ready for the war party. He took a pipe to Fast Whirlwind that he might pray over it. After he had purified himself through a sweat bath and prayers, Kills Many Enemies asked several young men with war experience to a feast, and all accepted his invitation to join the party. Four days after the feast they set out, with enough pemmican to last for a moon, and protected by the medicines hung around their necks. At the rear came Steals Horses who was allowed to go only in the minor capacity of moccasin bearer.

They were a gay group as they rode along talking over other war parties and great dangers of the past. They were in no hurry. For many sleeps they camped, now by the side of Black Tail Deer Creek, again near Porcupine Hill, as they approached closer and closer the camp grounds of the enemy. At night the warriors smoked around the fire and amused themselves by

The boy was sent out alone in the darkness to bring water

testing the courage of Steals Horses. The boy was sent out alone
in the darkness to a distant creek to bring water, while the braves
hooted like owls and made rustling sounds to frighten him. But
Steals Horses knew that all young boys were thus tested and
though he was frightened by the strange noises and the thought
that enemies might be lurking about, yet he went obediently
to the creek and trudged stolidly back with the water.

And at last, one day at the setting of the sun, a scout rode into
camp with news of the enemy. With a sharp pointed stick he
drew on the ground a map of the valley in which the Crows
were camped, showing the location of the tipis — more than a
hundred, he reported — and the grazing grounds of the horses.
Because the ponies were untethered, it was evident the Crows
were not expecting trouble. Knowing that the size of the camp
would make a general attack impossible, Kills Many Enemies,
with his lieutenants, worked out a plan to outwit their foes.

Just before dawn, two warriors, leaving their horses behind, crept quietly into the Crow village, herded together as many of the grazing ponies as they could, and led them off in the direction of their own camp. After allowing enough time for them to get away, Kills Many Enemies ordered two other braves to stampede the remaining horses. The chosen two, shouting the hair-raising war cry, were soon chasing the frightened Crow ponies away from the grounds and, as if the shouts were a signal, armed warriors came running from the tipis. With the appearance of the enemy, the Sioux braves, certain they would be pursued, rode back to join their comrades.

Waiting in ambush, Kills Many Enemies shrewdly divided his men into two groups which remained hidden on either side of the great valley. As a small party of Crow braves came galloping down in pursuit of the Oglalas, he signalled his warriors to close in around them. And soon the quiet of the day was shattered by the whirr of flying arrows, war yells, and the groans of the injured and dying.

The ambush had succeeded even beyond the hopes of Kills Many Enemies. He and his men quickly counted coup by touching the bodies of their foes, but he forbade them to take scalps. There was not time enough. Even now other Crow warriors were leaping to their recaptured horses to take up the fight. So Kills Many Enemies gave the order to retreat at once with the wounded.

Yet he himself delayed. The picture of Red Elk, wide-eyed with admiration, rose before him and, though his better judgment urged him to leave, his desire for glory was so strong that he could not resist the temptation to get scalps. But he had time to take only one before the Crow braves came pouring over the top of the hill. The young man waved the scalp, whooped in defiance, and leaped to his horse, lashing it to furious speed.

As he rode he shouted and sang in the best Sioux tradition of bravery, but in truth he was desperately afraid. The pounding hoofs of the pursuing horses were no louder in his ears than the wild beating of his heart. He had delayed too long. If only he could catch up with his men there would be some chance for him. He did not want to die — not now when life promised so much. More earnestly than he had ever done in all his winters he prayed to the Wakan Tanka, vowing to give the Sun Dance if, by some miracle, the Great Mysterious saved him. But his prayer was cut short by an arrow and Kills Many Enemies, sorely wounded, slumped over his horse which sped on to rejoin the retreating band.

After long days of weary travel during which they ministered as best they could to the wounded hero, the victorious party returned to a waiting people and to a camp at once merry and sad. There was a victory dance for the braves and many received new names. But from the tipi of one who had been killed a pathetic wailing could be heard, and his women went about with close-cropped hair, their long buckskin dresses covering gashed legs. The dead warrior had been dressed and painted, wrapped in a robe, and, followed by a procession of mourners, carried to a distant hill and placed on a scaffold there. In keeping with tribal custom, the mourning family honored the memory of its dead by publicly giving away most of their belongings so that now their tipi was almost bare.

While the mourners wept and the others gloated over the victory, in Standing Buffalo's tipi Kills Many Enemies lay near death from loss of blood and the pain of his wound. His father had lost no time in securing the services of Spotted Cloud, a medicine man of the bear cult, for only those men who had seen and talked with bears in their vision quests had power to heal wounds. Spotted Cloud, dressed in his bear costume, quickly spread the powerful bear medicine on a bed of sage and sang four songs, accompanied by the drumming and singing of his assistants. He repeated his vision and prayed to it, chanting, 'Great Holy, all is done as you command.' And he smoked the medicine pipe and gave his secret treatment to the youth. By the time the healers had partaken of the feast prepared for them and had left with their fee of robes and tools and ornaments, it was clear even to his anxious family that the shaman had saved the young man's life.

During his recovery the story of the battle was repeated again and again, up and down the camp — the shrewd leadership of the captain, the retreat, the arrival of the bleeding hero pursued by the Crow, and a miraculous escape directed by the wounded leader. The warriors told of the vow of Kills Many Enemies to give the Sun Dance if they were saved and the promise of others to dance with him. All over the camp the youth's praises were sung.

In honor of its brave member, the tokala society gave a dance and the warriors sang many songs for him. It was a proud moment for Kills Many Enemies when, after the feast, he rose to recite his deeds. In his hair he wore a red eagle feather for his wound and a white one for the coup he had won by touching the enemy brought down by his arrow. The light of the fire shone on his strong bronzed body and brightened the colored symbols painted on it. And the young brave told how he had earned the symbols, pointing to each mark as he spoke of the deed it represented — the yellow lines for his many coups, the white hoofprints for the horses he had taken, the black mark with red below it for his wound. At the close of the tokala dance, Kills Many Enemies proved himself generous as well as brave by the many things he gave away. Each time as he announced a gift — his beautifully embroidered moccasins, his buffalo robe,

Red Elk

three of his horses — the drums throbbed in praise. Honors were showered upon him. Even the Braves — the most important of all the soldier societies — invited him to become a member.

Heavy with his new importance, Kills Many Enemies proudly accepted the admiration of the people. And when the maiden Red Elk passed by, as she did very often now, her face newly painted and her freshly braided hair shining with bear's oil, he gazed through her as if she mattered not in the least to him. But he was young and full of life, and Red Elk was beautiful. So, when she had been sufficiently humbled by his indifference, he began to visit the girl's home — with the excuse of talking to her brother. On these visits Red Elk spoke no word but bustled about, working every minute of his stay so that he might see how capable she was and how good it would be for him if they should share a tipi. At an hour when it was likely she would be at the river drawing water, he would stroll past as if by accident, and after a time the evening came when, wrapped in his courting blanket, he met her and pulled it close about them both. Then it was he told her that he would give her brother two horses, that he could provide plenty of buffalo tongues for her, and that she was a good woman who would work well and bear sturdy sons. And it was agreed that after he had fulfilled his vow and given the Sun Dance she would come to him,

THE SUN DANCE

The prospect of the Sun Dance held no terrors now for Kills Many Enemies. He and the other youths who had also vowed to dance each chose an old man, called grandfather, to prepare them for the coming sacred act by sweat-bath rituals and vision quests. Kills Many Enemies, as leader, chose a powerful medicine man as his counsellor. Scouts were sent to other Oglala camps to announce that Kills Many Enemies of the Red Cloud Band was giving the Sun Dance three moons hence near Buffalo Hill and that all were invited to come.

In the tipi of Standing Buffalo there was now an altar on which a buffalo skull lay. Kills Many Enemies never touched this altar unless he first painted his hands in the sacred color red, and always before he ate he placed the best portion of food or drink on the altar as an offering to the gods. While the other men went out hunting and the societies organized war parties, he and those who were to dance with him remained at home, speaking little and meditating on the sacred task before them.

*Vision quest of Kills Many Enemies in preparation
for the Sun Dance*

One by one the Oglala groups arrived at the preliminary
camp site. The reunion with old friends brought much joyous
gossip as each band set up tipis in the camp circle in the place
to which it was entitled by tradition. Four days passed, filled
with prayers and dances. Then began the second four-day

period — the holy time. At sunrise an appointed body of scouts charged against the sacred site, shouting war cries and shooting arrows to drive the evil gods away, and when the herald proclaimed the grounds free from bad spirits, tipis were set up in the ceremonial camp.

The old chiefs who had seen many Sun Dances watched that all was done in the proper order. They saw the appointed women erect the Sacred Lodge in which each dancer's bed of sage was spread; the scout search out a growing cottonwood tree and mark it with round red spots on each of its four sides; the building of the Dance Lodge in the form of an open circle of forked poles pushed into the ground and covered with pine branches; the ceremonies of the capture and trimming of the tree; the binding of sweet grass, sage, and buffalo hair wrapped in chokecherry sticks to the fork at its top, its erection as the Sacred Pole, and the victory dance which made the floor smooth for the great dance to the Sun. While all these preparations were going on, the candidates had been spending their time in the Sacred Lodge, smoking and making incense with sage or sweet grass, or composing songs to be known as their own. Their minds purified by prayer and their bodies by sweat baths, they waited patiently for the great ordeal. Neither food nor drink would they have from the time they left the Sacred Lodge until the Sun Dance was over.

Before the sun appeared on the morning of the fourth holy day, men, women, and children, dressed in their most beautiful costumes, swarmed around the Dance Lodge to watch the approach of the procession of candidates. Kills Many Enemies was magnificent as he followed his grandfather out of the Sacred Lodge. A beautiful otterskin cape hung from his shoulders, and his bright red buckskin skirt blended with the red paint on his hands and feet. Anklets of rabbitskin showed beneath the long skirt. A wreath of sage sat proudly on his head. Carrying a buffalo head and looking neither to right nor left, Kills Many Enemies walked in measured step. Behind him, side by side with their grandfathers, marched the other dancers.

Four times the group passed around the shade of the Dance Lodge and each time, on reaching the entrance, they faced the sun and wailed. Then the procession entered and Kills Many Enemies, after three mock attempts, placed the buffalo head on the altar facing the Sacred Pole.

As ritual succeeded ritual — the final instructions to the dancers, the presentation of eagle-bone whistles to each of them, the buffalo dance, the piercing of children's ears — and the time came for the beginning of the Sun Dance, excitement swelled to frenzy. The slow beat of the drum and the chant of the singers changed from a soft, measured pattern to a torrential flood of sound. And with each quickening beat the suspense grew. Abruptly the drumming and the voices stopped. Then, with a thunderous war cry, a group of braves rushed upon the dancers, fighting a sham battle with seeming desperation. At last the attacking enemy were successful and the dancers lay on the ground before their captors.

The torture was to come now. The dancers lay motionless as the mock-enemy pierced holes in their flesh. Wooden sticks were thrust through these wounds. The less important dancers had buffalo skulls attached by leather thongs to the skewers in their backs. Others were tied to the Sacred Pole by thongs attached to the sticks thrust through the flesh of their breasts. Tumultuous sounds rose in deafening confusion — the throbbing beat of the drum, the chant of the war song, the encouraging cries of the audience, the wailing dirge of the dancers' relatives. Only the tortured ones were silent as stoically they submitted to the knife while maidens stood by delicately wiping away the blood with wisps of sweet grass.

In the Sun Dance Kills Many Enemies hung
suspended facing the east

Kills Many Enemies held his head high as he gave the signal for the dance to begin. He himself was lifted by the thongs which held him to the Pole until he could barely touch the ground and thus he hung suspended, facing the east. While their leader suffered the highest form of torture, others, tied to the Pole, stood in position, tirelessly bobbing up and down as, with each beat of the drum, they blew on their eagle bone whistles. And as the sun moved in the heavens, the eyes of the dancers followed it. Though weakened by lack of food and drink, and tortured by the burning sun and the pain of their wounds, they gave no sign of suffering. And the bleeding Kills Many Enemies, hanging from the Pole by his flesh, looked stoically down upon the spectators.

Throughout the long hot day, except for three rest periods, the group danced. And at last the time came for them to escape from their bonds. To cries of encouragement they pulled their bodies against the thongs, trying to jerk this way and that so their flesh would tear and release them. Two of the dancers fainted and their friends quickly took the skewers from their wounds and carried the weaklings away. Others, who could no longer struggle to free themselves, were helped by warriors who threw their arms about the waists of the sufferers and pulled them loose. But Kills Many Enemies fought on by himself, kicking out strongly as he hung from the Pole. And at last a desperate struggle ripped the flesh and skewers from his breast and back, and he fell to the ground. There he lay for a moment; then, to thunderous cries of admiration, slowly rose and walked to his place. The Sun Dance was over, and the leader had completed it with honor.

STAR OF THE PLAINS

Many stories have been passed down by word of mouth among the Plains Indians. Sitting about the campfire on long summer evenings, these tales and myths have been recited by skilled story-tellers until they have taken form almost as definite and exact as if they had been written. A favorite is the story of the son of a star who became the messiah of his people.

On the plains of the Dakotas, the story runs, a young girl, Katermu-win, had grown up among her sisters of the tribe and was just coming to womanhood. She knew well how to sew elk skins together to make a dress and to cover moccasins with cunning designs of porcupine quills. Long since she had given up her toys to help with the women's work. Some day, like her mother, she would be invited to join one or more of the women's societies, the tanners or the porcupine quill workers, take part in the women's feasts, and proudly display a new quill pattern or an elk skin rubbed soft and white.

After a day of feasting and ceremonies, Katermu-win was proclaimed a woman. That night she lay quietly in her father's tipi, troubled by the words the old women had spoken about her new womanhood and chafing at the thongs which had been bound about her thighs to keep her chaste. Through the tiny opening at the top of the tipi she gazed at a shining star and lay wondering what was beyond the great blanket of the sky. Was there a camp circle like that of her own people eternally ruled by the Wakan Tanka? And the stars, were they tall painted warriors of that far strange land, sentinels guarding the tipis of their people? Dreamily Katermu-win thought she would like to be married to the bright warrior star shining through the opening at the top of her tipi. And as she dreamed, swiftly she was carried to the sky to become the bride of the star.

Her life in the sky was much like that of her sisters on

earth, but light and beautiful as a dream. By night her star burned in the heavens, and by day he roamed the sky, hunting elk and buffalo so that his woman might have fine skins to wear and plenty of tongue to eat. Many moons passed and the happiness of Katermu-win grew, for soon she was to have a child.

All things in the land of the sky the young wife could have for her delight, save only that she was commanded never to dig up a prairie turnip when it was in full bloom. She gave her promise lightly, but each day as she walked among the blooming plants she wondered at this strange command. And her curiosity grew until she could resist no longer. Finding a beautifully flowering turnip, she dug it up and thereby dug her grave, for the floor of the heavens burst open and Katermu-win fell down and down to her death on the plains below.

A hawk saw her fall, and when from her broken body a babe emerged he was so troubled that he called a council of all the birds to decide what should be done with this miraculous child of a star. One after another the magpie, the buzzard, the eagle, and the hawk declined the care of the baby lest he die in their rough homes. Finally the child, named Falling Star, was given to the meadow lark because it was a kindly bird and its nest was safe and warm. And the Indians of the Plains say that because of pride in the child the meadow lark created its song. When Falling Star was but a lad he shot a buffalo calf, and the bird, taking the liver of the calf to a distant hill, sang proudly, 'Ptehinchila pinapi' (the calf's liver is rich). And ever since the call of the meadow lark has been the same, and if you listen carefully you will hear it — 'Ptehinchila pinapi, ptehinchila pinapi.'

The saga recites a series of adventures and marvels — 'Just-So Stories' of the Plains. Falling Star left the home of the meadow lark to help the people of his mother, and in every camp he visited he performed a miracle. In one camp he found the people oppressed by a tyrant who had the power of bringing death simply by pointing his finger at those who displeased him. And Falling Star stretched forth his hand, killing the despot and all his family save one son who escaped. That son is now known as Winter and every year, desolate and alone, he comes forth from his hiding place bringing the cold and snow with him.

At another encampment Falling Star found the people starving because a white crow frightened away the buffalo every time the Indians went to hunt. Here, too, he performed a miracle so that the Indians might eat and grow strong again. Changing himself into a buffalo calf, he captured the crow on his horns and took away its evil power. He hung it head downwards over a tipi fire until its feathers became black with soot and, strangling in the smoke, it could only cry, 'Caw, caw, caw.' Then, seeing it had become so poor a thing, Falling Star let it go; but from that day on all crows have been black and their only cry is the harsh and mournful 'caw.'

Just when the Indians needed him most the young saviour appeared, performed his miracles, and destroyed the mighty enemies of his people. Then he went away, promising that if ever they needed him he would come back.

More than a hundred years have passed since Falling Star left the Dakotas — lean years that have brought sorrow and defeat, strange years that have cluttered the ancient lands of the tribe with houses and hotels and stores, farms and fences, railroads and telegraph poles. The people who long ago wandered wild and free over the rolling plains now live penned in on a few thousand acres, forced to work for money to buy food which once was theirs for the taking. Many have studied the language and copied the strange customs of the white men and now teach in the new Indian schools or work in the Indian Office. Others, after scant training in white men's lessons, struggle to wrest a living from their arid allotments, from hauling freight by wagon, from building jobs offered by the government. And the old and weak are given their meager rations. In the summer many go to the near-by rodeos where they are given food in return for dressing up in paint and feathers and putting on travesties of their old war dances and sacred ceremonies to thrill the gaping tourist.

Life is no longer a dangerous and happy adventure. There are no more buffalo to hunt, no more enemy horses to steal, no war parties, no honor counts. All of the old hearty life in tipis is gone, and many of the unhappy Indians live in dark, boarded, dirt-floored houses. The loincloth and embroidered buckskin dresses no longer make a brilliant pageant. The picturesque dances and religious rites are remembered only by the old. The giving up of ancient taboos and courtship customs has brought license and disease. The once-strong bodies are eaten by dread scourges of syphilis and trachoma and tuberculosis. And, with ever-growing heartbreak, the old Indians see their children forsake the customs of their fathers, forget their language, consult white doctors rather than medicine men, and pray to the white god. The young are torn by conflict between the old traditions and the new life to which they try to adapt themselves. The aged are broken, embittered, powerless to halt the destruction of their life as a people.

The story of Falling Star's miracles has been handed down from generation to generation among his people. And even today, on the Pine Ridge Reservation in South Dakota, you may find an old man, seated cross-legged on the ground before his dreary house, talking over happy days that are gone and longing for the return of Falling Star.

'He promised to come back to us,' he chants. 'And when he does all will again be well for the Oglala.'

It is now but a dying hope. Things may again be well for the Oglala, but the old life will not return. If zest and joy ever come again to Indians on the Plains, the new life will be as different from the old as that was different from the life before the horse. It may yet be that in some strange new way Falling Star will return to save his people.

Dancing with fierce steps, the Senecas prepare for war

THE UNITED STATES
OF THE IROQUOIS

A YELL TORE THE STILL AIR of the forest by the Seneca River. In a little clearing dotted with bark houses, an Indian danced and shouted, stomping with swift high steps, brandishing his stone tomahawk, grimacing and jerking his painted body in stiff and threatening gestures. Suddenly running up to a great elm in the center of the clearing, he dashed the stone blade of his war hatchet into it and let out a terrific whoop — a long high call, sliding with a slow wail down the scale, then rushing up to end with a shriek on the same high note. Quickly other Indians joined him, dancing with the same fierce steps, shouting the same wild yells.

Before the furious dance began, the scene was peaceful enough on this summer day four hundred years ago in what is now central New York. From openings in the roofs of a dozen long bark houses smoke curled lazily upward. Encircling the village, a stoutly built stockade gave protection against attack. All about the clearing rose the primeval forest: giant hemlocks and graceful pines, tall oaks and elms and maples, sturdy walnut and hickory and butternut trees. Women could be seen in the fields beyond the village digging with wooden sticks or sitting beside the bark houses weaving baskets and shaping deer hides into moccasins, with their babies strapped to flat board cradles near-by.

As the dancers stomped and shouted, boys gathered eagerly, old men watched with approving nods, women turned from their tasks, stared and spoke earnestly among themselves. In a bursting chorus of yells the warriors stopped their dance. As the sun went down, feasting began and continued through the night. When dawn came the warriors made ready. Swiftly they tied bark armor about their bodies, crammed reed helmets on their heads, seized bows and arrows and clubs, and threw over their shoulders belts with pouches full of parched corn and maple sugar. Then they glided into the forest, one man stepping close behind another, fifty warriors in a single line. The Senecas were on the warpath.

Toward the end of summer the war parties would come back to their home clearings. Occasionally a party, wiped out to the last man in fierce combat, would be waited for in vain throughout the autumn and long winter. But almost always the bands came home glowing with victory, lacking only a few of their number, bringing many captives.

The fate of the prisoners was left to the women. If they decreed death, the prisoner was tied to a stake, tortured, and burned amid the taunts and jeers of the whole village. If they showed mercy, the captive was given a chance to prove himself worthy of adoption into the tribe. Naked, he ran the gauntlet to the house of the woman who had sponsored him, between rows made up of all the women and children of the village who beat him with whips and clubs. If he faltered or fell he was doomed to the stake as a weakling. If he made the run successfully he was a free man from the moment he reached the door of his new home; at once he ceased to be an enemy and thenceforth was treated with all the love and respect of a brother in the tribe.

Long pleasant hunts in the autumn succeeded the fierce war parties of the spring and summer. And in winter, with the harvests thriftily stored away, the villages settled down to long leisure, to the palaver of council meetings, to games and dances, to the long thrilling tales of the storytellers.

During the moon of Nisa (January) that same little clearing by the Seneca River, where but a few months before war whoops tore the air, showed a scene of sylvan quiet. Toward the end of a bright winter day men could be seen trudging in with deer trussed up by the legs to poles swung between their shoulders. Padding along on snowshoes made of tough sinew stretched across wooden frames (looking very much like huge tennis racquets) they followed well-worn trails along the ice and snow from the forest to the clearing. On the river bank old men sat dangling sinew strings into holes cut in the ice and shouting joyfully as they drew up fish. In the open space around the great elm tree, where in the summer the war dancers had worked themselves to a frenzy, laughing groups were now playing games.

At one spot a dozen men in warm deerskin coats and leggings and thick moccasins were busy at snow snake, a contest in throwing wooden javelins along an icy trough. Members of opposing teams kept up a din of shouts and laughter, cheering their champions at each throw, mocking the misfortunes of rival spears as they bounced along the rough ice. In an open space, teams of young men with crude racquets were tossing a hard buckskin ball, practising the popular summer game which is the forefather of modern lacrosse. On another patch of snow,

Seneca Indians playing games

boys were throwing javelins through rolling hoops and shouting
at the romping, barking dogs which could not keep from joining
this sport. Further away, groups of girls were kicking a ball of
deer hide stuffed with corn husks, and squealing with laughter
as they missed the ball and kicked one another's shins or fell
rolling in the snow.

As the sun dropped behind the dark pines the players and
fishermen gathered up their gear and wandered into the houses.
Most of the buildings were long halls sometimes more than a
hundred feet by sixteen or twenty-four feet across, made by
strapping great slabs of elm bark one above another within two
rows of posts. Inside these long houses, in a line down the center
of the hall, fires burned within stone hearths set at regular
intervals of about eight paces, the smoke curling out through
openings in the bark roofs. Many families lived in one house
and each fire was used in common by two to four of them.
Thus sixteen or twenty-four families might live in a long house
of four or six fires. The apartments were marked off by skins

On a winter afternoon

hung from the rafters and sometimes by a lattice woven of corn husks.

Beds or seats of logs and bark were built against the wall along both sides of the houses, and several feet above them ran an upper tier of shelves or bunks reached by ladders of notched poles. In every corner stood bark casks filled with parched corn, dried squashes, chunks of maple sugar, smoked meat and fish. Pits dug in the earthen floors, or in the fields outside, were stocked with corn, charred and carefully packed in husks so that it would keep for months. Hanging from the ceiling or stored on the bunks were the prized possessions of each family: bows and arrows and war clubs; rolls of tanned deerskin ready to be fashioned into shirts or moccasins, ash splints ready to be woven into baskets, long bright feathers, strings of shells and polished stones.

Within the walls of the houses there was a smoky warmth and, as the men came in from the snow and wind outside, they laid aside the heavy skins which formed their coats and blankets.

Soon the young men began games of chance, throwing like dice little disks carved from elk horn or buttons made of peach stones. The older men sat or lay on the low bunks as they waited for supper. Some of them filled little pipes with tobacco mixed with sumac leaves and contentedly added their smoke to the clouds that were filling the hall from the glowing hearths.

The women, busy with their cooking, paid little attention to the men. But as the outside shadows deepened, one after another of the women grunted out a call, and quickly the men and boys of her family took their places, sitting on mats and skins about her fire. The woman dipped a wooden ladle into the cooking pot and poured steaming hominy into the bark dish which each man held. She passed them chunks of roast venison and pieces of corn bread, and perchance, at the end of the meal, little cakes made of corn meal, maple sugar, and hickory nuts, which always called forth grunts of 'oguhoh' (delicious).

Scarcely would the men have finished eating on most winter evenings when there would be a rush to gather around the storyteller. The women and girls would quickly devour the food left by the men, hastily clean up the remains, and come to join the circle. People would crowd in from other houses, and unless rival orators were holding forth in other halls, the whole village would gather round. Far into the winter night the storyteller, in language that had become so fixed by tradition that it was almost a chant, would recite myths and fables, histories of the tribe, tall tales of ancient heroes.

The scenes in this Seneca village were duplicated with only slight variations throughout the five nations of Iroquois people who lived in the woodlands of central New York: the Mohawks, farthest east, between the Mohawk River and the Adirondack Mountains; the Oneidas, next westward, around Oneida Lake

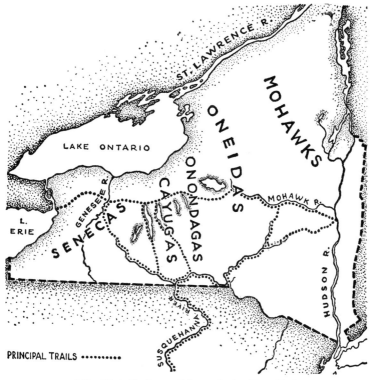

The Five Nations of Iroquois in New York

and the eastern tip of Lake Ontario; the Onondagas, in the
center; the Cayugas, farther westward around the shores of
Cayuga Lake; and the Senecas, living about the lake and river
of their name and on westward to the Genesee River. All these
Iroquois people had much in common. They were all of the
same blood and spoke the same basic language. They worshipped the same Great Spirit through similar ceremonies.
They lived close together. They had a similar social organization and mode of life.

CLANS AND CUSTOMS

The Iroquois, like the Pueblos and many other Indians, built their social structure on clans. Among the Iroquois these clans were made up of families which traced their descent through the female line. Thus a clan consisted of the original mother, her children, her daughter's children, and all the descendants through the women. Since marriage was not permitted between members of the same clan, a man had to look outside for a wife. Thus a man was never of the same clan as his own children since they followed their mother.

This marriage law, called exogamy (out-of-the-group), is a more rigid pattern than ours. In Europe and modern America we generally put a taboo on marriage between near relatives but have no set form of computing relationship beyond close blood ties. The Iroquois, and other people who followed the exogamous clan pattern, regarded all members of a clan as one family and therefore not proper marriage mates. A man was free to marry any woman who was not of his mother's clan. But he could not marry a member of his own clan, however distant the blood relationship.

The clans were named for familiar animals or birds — bear, wolf, turtle, heron, eel — which scholars commonly refer to as the totems of the clans, and each Iroquois house had its totem carved or painted above the door.[1] The clans ran throughout the five nations, though not all clans were found in every nation. Members of the same clan regarded themselves as brothers wherever they lived. A Mohawk of the Wolf clan felt

---

[1] Certain tribes of the Pacific Coast carved images of their totems on beautiful cedar door posts, and totem poles with carvings of the heraldry and history of given families are among the interesting objects of art of the northwest Indians. Certain non-Indian tribes outside America have complicated rules about the totems for which their clans are named, including in some cases a taboo against eating the flesh of the totem animal. But with the Iroquois there is little evidence of any special regard for the animals which furnished the clan names.

as much a brother to a Wolf clansman of the Senecas as if they were children of the same parents; when visiting Seneca territory he would go at once to a house bearing the wolf totem and be sure of a warm family welcome.

The clans in each village belonged to one or the other of two major divisions which we call moities or phratries. The function of these groups was largely social: in games the Iroquois played and bet as phratries; and at important funerals the phrators of the dead person mourned while the other phratry conducted the ceremonies. Sometimes in the case of murder, the clan of the murderer appealed to its brother clans to act as a body in persuading the phratry of the victim's family to condone the crime.

Among the Iroquois even more than with most Indians, woman was the worker. She tilled the soil and gathered the crops. She helped to fell the trees and build the lodge. She tanned the hides of the animals her men killed and made from them the clothes and covers for her family. She patiently and skilfully worked the quills of porcupines into intricate designs to decorate their costumes. She took the earth and moulded it into crude pots. She gathered corn husks or flags or splint and braided them into fine baskets. With the bark her husband peeled from the trees, she made saucers and bowls and barrels, trays for preparing bread, tubs for making sugar, straps to carry burdens which all day long were on her patient back. She gathered sap from the maple for sugar and seeds from the sunflower for bread. She pounded corn. She cooked. She cared for the children.

Along with all these labors, women had a higher place in social life and public affairs than was usual among Indians. When she married, the husband usually came to live in the house of her clan and was a guest in her lodge, welcome only so long as he furnished game and proved himself acceptable. The crops and the house were hers. Children belonged to her clan and on her death all her possessions went to them, while the widower returned to the lodge of his parents. Older women achieved great authority in their clans and often dictated the choice of chiefs and sachems. Women were equally represented among the religious authorities, the Keepers of the Faith, and two women of each community were joint matrons of the healing society known as the Company of Faces. While much of her political authority was indirect, the woman exercised a deciding voice in many important matters of public life. If a woman was murdered the injured family was entitled to twice as much atonement as for a man. In the ceremonies of mourning for a dead chief, the people consoled themselves with the thought that it would have been far worse to lose a woman: 'He who has worked for us has gone afar off... But it is still harder when a woman dies, because with her the line is lost.'

Religion and social custom were so interwoven that it was impossible to separate them. Law or good behavior with the Iroquois was supported equally by social usage and sacred lore. In fact most rules of conduct were not thought of as laws or commandments but simply as the ways all decent people acted. The punishment for most faults was simply that people would not think well of you. And the threat of disfavor did more to control conduct than all our modern fines and prisons.

A few crimes were subject to special punishments. For adultery the woman was publicly whipped. In case of murder the offender was killed by members of the injured family unless his clan could persuade them to pardon him while he himself confessed his sin and offered apology and payment. Because of the dread of evil spirits, witchcraft was regarded as the most terrible crime. If a person was caught putting a curse on anyone or attempting magic dealings with evil spirits, he might be killed by the beholder or brought before the council. Oddly, to our way of thinking, a confession of his sin and a promise to live righteously thereafter brought pardon. On the other hand, a denial of guilt (if the charge was supported by more than one witness) brought death.

The confession of sins was widely practised. On public occasions, such as autumn festivals, ceremonial dances, or even council meetings, men and women recited their misdeeds. They did not tell their sins to priests or undertake any penance. They simply cleared their souls of the feeling of guilt through confession and the resolve to do better in future.

In order to win divine favor and gain protection from evil, the Iroquois purified themselves by fasting and sweat baths. Medicine men were called in to cure sickness and drive out evils by chants and rituals. Certain severe illnesses were thought to be caused by a mind troubled by desire for some special object. In these cases there could be no cure until the patient got what he wanted. Thus a dying man was sometimes surrounded by knives, bows and arrows, ornaments, all manner of objects. If he recovered he felt he owed his life to the last thing brought and ever afterward held that object in high esteem. If he died his family mourned that they had failed to find the one thing his spirit craved.

Other ailments were cured by a secret healing society known as the Company of Faces or the Falseface Band. Certain ills — nosebleed, toothache, eye troubles — were supposed to be brought by hideous, disembodied faces which flew about spreading pestilence. To ward off these evil spirits, a group of people in each village masked themselves in grotesque falsefaces more hideous than the demons they were fighting. When a sick person dreamed of a Falseface, he told the mistress of the Band

and had a feast prepared. Then, in full force, led by the woman and wearing their fantastic masks, the Falsefaces marched into the lodge of the patient. Stirring the ashes of the fire and sprinkling them over the head of the sick man, they performed the Falseface dance in which the patient joined. As only the mistress of the Band knew the members, who never unmasked in public or even among themselves, the feast had to be carried away to be eaten by each Falseface in privacy.

When an Iroquois died his body, richly clothed and painted, was carried to a distant spot, placed on a bark scaffold, and surrounded with food, bows and arrows, pipe and tobacco. It was thought that the spirit hovered near the body for several days, so every night for half a moon a fire was built near the scaffold in order that the man's soul might prepare its food. Sometimes a bird was freed above the body to carry the spirit to

When an Iroquois died his body was placed on a bark scaffold

heaven. Since the journey from the earth to the sky took a full year, that was the period of mourning. When the body was wasted to a skeleton, the bones were reverently gathered and stored in the bark house of his clan.

The Iroquois believed in a Great Spirit and an Evil Spirit, twin brothers born of the daughter of a woman from the sky. The good brother created man, the sun, moon, and stars, and all useful plants and animals. The evil one, jealous of his twin, tried to undo all the good by making poisonous plants and reptiles, discord and disease. Both the Great Spirit and the Evil Spirit had a corps of assistants who helped them in their work. Among the good helpers were He-no, the Thunderer, who controlled the rain; the Spirit of the Winds, an old man living in the west who when restless caused winds to blow and storms to rage, and the Three Sisters, the spirits of maize and beans and squashes, who loved one another so dearly that even the crops named after them grew better when planted together. Almost every object of nature was watched over by a guardian spirit or was subject to corruption by an evil force. In their natural reverence the Iroquois had no word or phrase which could express profanity to any of the spiritual forces.

The smoke of burning tobacco carried the people's prayers heavenward as they chanted: 'Great Spirit, master of all things visible and invisible; Great Spirit, master of other spirits, whether good or evil, command the good spirits to favor your children; command the evil spirits to keep at a distance from us.' In their public religious ceremonies they took care to offer thanks not only to the Great Spirit but to all his subordinates.

Festivals regularly held in the various villages attracted visitors from all the near-by region. These popular gatherings were held throughout the year, beginning with the maple dance of early spring and reaching a climax in the new year's ceremonies, the chief festival of the Iroquois calendar. These were times for prayers and thanksgiving, for feasts and games and dances.

But the greatest festival to the Iroquois braves was war. They made war on Indians far and near and, in the early days, battled among themselves as ferociously as they fought strangers. They knew the woods so well that they supplied their needs for months on the warpath from the abundant deer and quail and fish of the eastern woodlands. They were so skilful and stealthy that they would steal up on villages or enemy bands and turn the serenity of the bright morning into wild terror by their sudden war whoops. Impatient of the scattered warfare of bows and arrows, they rushed upon their enemies, killing scores and hundreds in close combat with their deadly hatchets and war clubs. Proud, brave, resourceful, the Iroquois warriors loved adventure, welcomed danger, laughed at pain. Even death held slight terror, for they sang, 'Better to be broken like a young oak in the hurricane than wait for rot to set in and eat up the heart.'

THE IROQUOIS LEAGUE OF NATIONS

The Iroquois battled so fiercely and so continuously that there was danger that the nations would be ruined by their bitter warfare. Among the favorite tales of the old storytellers were accounts of these early wars and the efforts of a hero — Hiawatha — to bring peace among his people by forming a great league of nations.

The name Hiawatha has been made familiar to modern Americans through Longfellow's poem. While Longfellow mingled the stories of many tribes to make a general saga of Indian life, and even cast his chief character as a Chippewa rather than an Iroquois, his poem took its inspiration from the great folk hero of the Iroquois and has about it the atmosphere of the woodland storytellers.

All stories agree that a wise man (which is what the word Hiawatha means), seeing the warring tribes of the Iroquois all at one another's throats, planned a league that would unite the nations and bring peace. He dreamed and planned and preached, as Longfellow's poem says,

> Not for greater skill in hunting,
> Not for greater craft in fishing,
> Not for triumph in the battle,
> Nor renown among the warriors,
> But for profit of the people,
> For advantage of the Nations.

The greatest obstacle to the union was Atotarho, another folk hero of majestic outline. He is said to have had snakes growing from his mighty head, and to have used the skulls of his enemies as dishes and spoons, to have been so fierce that no man could stand against him, so strong that single-handed he had brought his nation, the Onondagas, to the top of the struggling, warring heap of North American Indians. Hiawatha pled with Atotarho to make a league with his brother nations. Atotarho would have none of it. He killed all Hiawatha's brothers and threatened to kill him if he did not cease his talk of peace and union.

But nothing could stop the dreamer. He went eastward to the land of the Mohawks, in an odyssey lovingly dwelt on by the storytellers, climbing mountains, guiding his canoe through wild and surging waters, beating and tearing his way through dense forests, until worn and weary he found the wise Mohawk chief, Dekanawida. That intelligent leader at once saw the need for union and helped Hiawatha gain the support of his nation and of the near-by Oneidas. In time the Cayugas and Senecas were also persuaded to join in a league of Iroquois peoples. With the backing of these nations, Hiawatha came again to the Onondagas. He cajoled and flattered Atotarho,

*Guiding his canoe through wild and surging waters, Hiawatha
went eastward to the land of the Mohawks*

promising that his nation should have the largest number of sachems in the council and that he and his successors for all time should hold the most honored name in the league. Finally he persuaded the tyrant to throw in his lot with the union. In the figurative language of the storytellers, Hiawatha combed the snakes from Atotarho's hair.

Hiawatha's dream was that all the Iroquois tribes and nations, which were spread over a large part of northeastern America, would unite to form a great league, cease fighting among themselves, possibly even establish a universal peace for all his world. But only those five nations joined which were closely related by blood and lived near together in central New York. While many Iroquois-speaking peoples were left outside, the term Iroquois as used today generally refers to those five nations which formed the League. The people called their union 'Kanonghsyonny' (house drawn out). In their imagery it was simply an extension of their own long houses, and they referred to themselves as 'The People of the Long House.'

'All these things happened long ago,' the stories say, and it is hard to set exact dates to these early deeds. Scholars today think the League of the Iroquois may have been started as early as five hundred years ago; it is known to have been operating in some form in the early fifteen hundreds; Lewis H. Morgan, an early student of the Iroquois, sets the date of complete organization at 1570.

The League was a wise and effective union. It was ruled by a council of fifty sachems, all equal in rank and authority, who combined in themselves all the powers of government. A fixed number of sachems were assigned to each nation and these were elected within that nation by the several clans.

No wiser method could have been found to hold the League in an indissoluble union. It wove into a single texture the warp of the several nations and the woof of the various clans. If the delegates of one nation wanted to thwart the League, they would have to go against their clansmen, their brothers in the other nations. If one clan was disgruntled it would not dare to act against the interests of its neighbors in the villages and nations where its members lived.

The post of sachem was both hereditary and elective: hereditary in the clan and nation, for the office remained forever within that group; elective since at the death of the sachem any member of his clan within the given nation could be chosen to replace him. Sachemship could never go from father to son since the son belonged to a different clan, that of his mother. The office might go to a brother or to the son of a sister. It was intended that the successor of a sachem be the man of the clan and nation best fitted to govern 'for the profit of the people, the advantage of the nations,' regardless of close ties to a previous holder. But actually a tendency developed to pass office down within certain exalted families. The selections by the clan and nation had to be confirmed by the League, which had as one of its most solemn ceremonies the 'raising up' of the nominees. The sachems not only sat on the council of the League, but were the chief figures in the councils of their own clans and their own nations.[1]

The League gave unity and stability to Iroquois life yet it left the several nations independent in all matters which did not vitally affect the commonweal, and it left the villages and individual families as free as they ever were in their daily lives and customs.

---

[1] If we had this system we would elect a single group of leaders who would comprise the several state legislatures and also act all together to form the United States Congress. In addition, these same leaders would be representatives of other aspects of our life which run in common through all the states, such as national fraternal orders, trade unions, religious denominations, which all taken together might approach the close interstate ties of the Iroquois clans.

Oddly enough, to our way of thinking, there were no war chiefs among the central governors and the League did not undertake to control wars — other than to decree peace among its own members. War was the zest of life to the Iroquois, just as business and the making of money have been regarded as the zest of life to modern Americans. The Iroquois brave cherished freedom and independence in his fighting, just as we do in our business. It is true that when war became a more complex matter with the coming of the white men, two war counsellors were appointed by the League, just as in the modern world of great corporations and international trade our governments have had to regulate business. But the Iroquois counsellors were supervisors, not generals. They regulated and restrained expeditions that might embroil the League as a whole, arranged treaties with important foreign nations, supervised the conquered people. They did not take away the initiative or curb the cherished rights of any man or any group to make war when or how he pleased. One may imagine Iroquois braves begrudging even regulation in this dearest realm of activity, orating on the God-given right of a man to fight and die in his own way regardless of the commonweal, denouncing the softness that must come when government interfered in any way with private initiative and free competition.

The meetings of the League council were great public festivals as well as political sessions. The council usually met each autumn near Onondaga Lake which was central to the whole realm. But sessions of the council might be called at any time by the sachems of any nation and these special meetings were held within the territory of the nation calling them. The calls went out by messengers running on the well-worn trails which stretched across the realm east and west from the Hudson to Lake Erie, north and south through the valley of the Susquehanna, and reaching remote villages by a hundred branching trails. Relays of runners are reported to have covered a hundred miles in a day and to have carried messages from the Mohawks in the east clear to the Senecas in the west in less than three days.

As soon as the call to the council was spread by these swift runners, men, women, and children began to pack up and start on the trek, through forests, around lakes, down streams, often two hundred miles or more to the chosen spot. Hundreds would assemble from every part of the realm. Unity among the nations was strengthened by these great congresses in which the people as a whole met in council, listened to the debates of their governors, were free to speak before the council, took part in the dances which followed, gossiped, played games, got acquainted with brothers from remote villages around the great council fire.

One of the formal duties of the League was to mourn sachems who had died and to raise up their successors. At the sessions of a 'mourning council' long speeches of condolence were made and then with a shout the new sachem was brought forward. 'The king is dead; long live the king.'

The sachems were installed with recitals of the history and principles of the League. The laws were repeated from strings of wampum, shells of various colors woven together on sinew into figures which had special meanings. Each fact or law was associated with a particular string — the only formal records the Iroquois had. They spoke of laws or treaties as having been 'talked into' the wampum, and these archives were interpreted by persons specially versed in wampum lore. No agreement was regarded as binding unless it was accompanied by a string of wampum which then became a sacred bond. The reciting of agreements and laws from the historic wampum belts was a patriotic ceremony, instructive alike to the new sachem and to the great mass of people who listened reverently.

When questions came before the council they were presented in an oration by a delegate of the nation which had brought up the proposal or which stood sponsor for a petition from an alien group. After the proposal was stated anyone was free to speak his mind. But the Iroquois were so ceremonious that, instead of a lot of helter-skelter speaking, groups chose skilled orators to present their views. Although the council alone made the decisions, the people's orators were listened to with attention and doubtless often influenced the vote. The modern American custom of listening to speeches has an honorable ancestry among the Iroquois who would sit for hours, nodding, applauding, laughing, as orators harangued on all subjects. A fluent tongue could sway them easily. Eloquence was as sure a path to glory as arms.

When the formal business of the council was finished, days and nights were given over to social fellowship. The whole congress, sachems and people alike, would stay on for a week or more, taking part in sacred dances, playing in athletic contests, gambling, feasting, listening to storytellers, enjoying themselves in the hearty friendliness of camp life.

RISE AND FALL OF THE IROQUOIS

With the formation of the League, the Iroquois became the most formidable force in eastern North America. They had always been fierce warriors. Now that their war parties were turned from neighborhood strife and united in great expeditions against outside nations, they were even more powerful. With the coming of the Dutch to the Hudson and of the French to the St. Lawrence, the Iroquois learned about firearms, far more deadly than arrows or war clubs. Quickly taking up

At the League councils orators were listened to with attention

these new weapons, they made themselves a terror throughout the region.

For a hundred years from 1600 to 1700, the Iroquois were almost continuously waging war. Hiawatha's dream of universal peace long forgotten, they swooped down on alien tribes at their borders and sometimes even hundreds of miles distant. They wiped out their ancient enemies of the St. Lawrence: the Hurons and many Algonquian tribes. They smashed the Eries and the confederated Neutrals of the Great Lakes. They conquered the Delawares and 'made women of them.' They subdued all the neighboring tribes down the Susquehanna and along the southern ranges of the Appalachian Mountains. They attacked the Cherokees far south in what is now Georgia and Alabama. Their raiding parties reached as far west as the Black Hills of the Dakotas and southwest to the Gulf of Mexico. They established their sovereignty throughout the whole region from the Hudson and Lake Champlain on the east to Lake Superior and the Mississippi River on the west, from the St. Lawrence on the north far south to the Tennessee Valley.

The Iroquois during the century from 1600 to 1700 had established a military empire larger in territory than that of Rome at its greatest period. They were perhaps ready to begin the consolidation of that empire, to develop the arts of peace as they had so successfully pursued the arts of war. But they were never given the chance. Aggressors stronger than they came on the scene. The empire they might have developed was built by others.

It is impossible to set with any accuracy the numbers of the Iroquois at their heyday. Guesses run all the way from seventeen thousand to seventy thousand. A conservative estimate places the total population of the Five Nations in 1650 at about twenty-five thousand. At most they were an astonishingly small number, judged by modern populations or by the influence they wielded in their time. They were essentially hunters who were beginning to farm but who still regarded crops as only a supplement to game. It is likely that with the continued development of their agriculture, together with the consolidation of their empire, they would have increased greatly in population. But that chance also was denied them by the surging populations of white men that overwhelmed them.

The coming of the white men seemed at first a boon to the Iroquois. They obtained from the newcomers the magic firearms which helped them to subdue their enemies. They engaged in an active fur trade with the Dutch and French which brought what seemed like fresh wealth and prosperity. They were far enough removed from the first colonies to feel little pressure from them, and they were skilful in playing off the enmities of the English and French and Dutch to what seemed like their own advantage.

But these gains were brief and false. While firearms made it possible for them to conquer enemies, these expeditions cost the lives of many of the finest Iroquois at the prime of life who could ill be spared from their sparse population. Brandy and rum, which with firearms were the chief articles bartered with the Indians for their furs, proved a terrible curse. The Iroquois, like other Indians, quickly crumbled under alcohol. Their statesmen and orators, minds befuddled and tongues thickened by drink, lost their power to think wisely and persuade elo-quently. Weakened by brandy and rum, their warriors lost their cunning, and the whole population became an easy prey to the new diseases. The French missionaries lured many away to distant settlements and set brother against brother in religion, sometimes even in war. By joining in the wars between the English and the French, the Iroquois became involved in a struggle which they did not understand, between forces which in the end destroyed them.

In 1715 the Tuscaroras, driven out of North Carolina by the white settlers, sought refuge with their relatives the Iroquois and were admitted to the confederacy as the sixth nation, though they were never allowed membership on the League council. This gave added numbers to the dwindling population. But the League was not destined to live much longer. It almost perished in the struggle between France and England in 1754 and received its death blow in the Revolution.

When the war between England and the colonists began, both sides pled with the Iroquois — the English for their assistance, the colonists for their neutrality. The Oneidas refused to be drawn into the quarrel and assured the Governor of Connecticut that they would remain neutral, stating, 'Brothers, possess your minds in peace respecting us Indians. We cannot meddle in this dispute between two brothers. The quarrel seems to be unnatural. You are two brothers of one blood. We are unwilling to join on either side in such a contest for we bear an equal affection for both Old and New England.'

The question finally came before the League council, but though four of the tribes voted to side with the English, the Oneidas staunchly refused to fight. According to the laws of the League, this lack of unanimity should have ended the matter. Instead, the council made an exception. It ruled that in this case each nation could follow its own inclination, fighting or not as it deemed best. For the first time in more than two hundred years a solemn League law was broken, the union severed.

During the war the Iroquois suffered frightful losses at the hands of the colonial army which swept over their country, burning their homes and destroying their growing crops. Even the English forgot them, for when the treaty of peace was signed in 1783, they did not bother to see that any provision was made for their faithful allies.

As Hiawatha had foreseen when

> ... a darker, drearier vision
> Passed before me, vague and cloud-like;
> I beheld our nations scattered,
> All forgetful of my counsels,
> Weakened, warring with each other;
> Saw the remnants of our people
> Sweeping westward, wild and woeful,
> Like the cloud-rack of a tempest,
> Like the withered leaves of autumn.

The six tribes were scattered to the four winds. The Mohawks and Cayugas left their ancient homes to live in Ontario, though some of the Cayugas moved to Wisconsin and Ohio. The Oneidas were forced to yield territory after territory until only a small reservation remained to them in New York. Some went to Canada, while others made their homes in Wisconsin. Most of the Onondagas remained in New York, but some removed to Canada and still others to the west. The Senecas had to cede away their lands until only three tiny reservations in New York remained to them.

So ended the great League. The once closely-knit tribes were torn asunder, the voice of the orator was heard no more, and the great council fire died down never to be rekindled. The birth of the white man's United States brought death to the united states of the Iroquois.

THE PUEBLOS OF
THE SOUTHWEST

AROUND THE ANCIENT Indian villages by the Rio Grande, July was the time for great rabbit hunts. After priests had prayed before a sacred bonfire, the whole village poured out and scoured the plains for the little animals which furnished delicious meat and useful furs, and which if left living in too great numbers ate up the village crops. Forming a great circle, the Indians slowly closed in, beating the bushes until they had penned in hundreds of rabbits which were then killed by clubs and stones or even caught in the hands of clever hunters. But the rabbits were sly and nimble. It was not easy to trap them, and even when cornered it required skill to catch them. Men, women, and children had great sport in these hunts. Those who came home laden with game were happy and boastful. Those who got none were the butt of boisterous jokes.

[1] This story of old Pueblo life was suggested by incidents in the classic novel of the Southwest, *The Delight Makers*, by A. F. Bandelier. While the descriptions of ancient customs are based on modern knowledge which goes far beyond the earlier studies of Bandelier, the story follows one of the themes of *The Delight Makers*, with the courteous permission of the publishers, Dodd, Mead & Company.

As the sun was going down on such a hunt outside the village
of Tyuonyi some five hundred years ago, the people began to
troop homeward. Boys and girls ran about with happy cries.
Men shouted and laughed. Even women, rejoicing in the
license of the festival, put aside their usual reticence and flung
boasts and taunts back and forth as loudly as the men.

'Ho, great warrior, is that an elk you have?' cried a girl whose
arms were laden with rabbits to a boy whose sole trophy was the
upper part of a carcass which had been broken clean in two by
his clumsy stone.

'Be quiet, water mole,' the boy answered, and made a lunge
to grab her hair.

She ran squealing and giggling to the protection of two older
women, and, peering around their shoulders, jeered, 'Brave
warrior, fierce panther!' Then, sticking out her tongue, she
hissed, 'Big buck crow!' and darted into the midst of a whole
group of women who, closing about her, carried on her
taunts.

Among the jeering, laughing crowd, two women stood together. One, the frail Say Koitza (Mrs. Say or the woman Say),
a respected mother in the pueblo, had no rabbits. The other,
Shuama, strong and lithe as the panther for which she was
named, proudly displayed her catch. She must have been well
past thirty — old age for an Indian woman — but her limbs
were well formed and strong, her face handsome, her dark eyes
sparkling.

Shuama stiffened as she saw the man Tyope, hissed 'Carrion
crow,' and started toward him. But her companion pulled at
her arm, pleading gently, 'This is a good day. Let us not spoil
it by bitterness. It is not well to mix hate with joy. Come home.'

As the two women walked northward along the tableland,
which in the Southwest is called a mesa, they came suddenly to

As the two women walked home from the rabbit hunt
they passed fields of young maize

a deep valley through which ran a small clear stream. Beyond
this rose a yellow cliff about two hundred feet high, topped with
tall jagged turrets of bare stone. As they walked up the valley,
they passed fields of young bushy maize plants and little gardens
of beans and squashes. The valley narrowed, and strange piles
of rock and earth appeared, tier upon tier of little stone and
mud rooms, the great straggling apartment houses of the various
clans of the village. They glimpsed dozens of little oblong holes
in the cliff itself — openings leading to rooms which had been
carved out of the soft pumice of the cliffside.

Before one of these holes Shuama paused and, lifting a coarsely
woven cotton cloth which covered the opening, stepped into
her home, one of the cliff dwellings of her people, the Water
clan. Seeing that her frail companion was tired and knowing

that she had been ill of a fever for many moons, Shuama asked
her in to rest before going on to her home far up the valley.
The women found themselves in a room about ten feet square
which seemed dark and cool as they stepped from the glare of
the setting sun outside. Shuama pushed a neat roll of skins
forward for her companion to sit on and, dipping a gourd into
an earthen pot of water, handed her a drink, while she herself
sat down on the earth floor, her feet stretched comfortably out
before her. For a long time the women sat quietly, visiting
without a word. Then Say rose, uttered a low 'hoya' of thanks,
and pushed aside the curtain of the doorway.

As she stooped and clambered out of the small opening,
Shuama, without moving from her seat on the floor, looked up
and said, 'It may be I can help your sickness. I will come to
your house at dark.'

'Raua' (good), answered Say. 'My man will be at the kiva.
I will be alone.'

Say walked on alone, beyond green fields and gardens where
the valley had opened into a wide level bed, on past rows of
houses and clusters of little openings in the cliff, until, in the
course of half a mile of walking beside the stream, she came to
a wide shelf of earth which jutted out between the cliff and the
river. Here stood the largest of the apartment houses of the
village, a rough coliseum of stone and earth with walls two and
three stories high. From the courtyard within this coliseum
houses rose in tiers, the upper stories set back eight or ten feet
from those below, so that the roofs of the lower tiers served as
balconies or terraces for the houses above. Three clans lived
in this enclosure, the houses of each forming one section of the
uneven structure. In the central courtyard three large cylinders
of plaster rose about four feet above the level of the ground and
against the inside of these holes leaned notched poles, ladders

Three clans lived in this huge coliseum

leading down to caverns which were the kivas, the clubhouses of the men, the town halls, the sacred grottos of societies and clans.

Say crossed the courtyard to the far wall of the coliseum which housed her clan, the Gourd people. She climbed a notched log which led to a terrace made by the roofs of the first tier of houses and, putting aside a deerskin which hung before her doorway, she entered her home. At once she went to a little niche in the side wall and took from a brightly decorated bowl a handful of holy meal. This she scattered in the six sacred directions: east, north, west, south, upward toward the heavens, and downward to the earth. Then, though she was tired and weak from her recent fever, she went stolidly about her household tasks.

Going to the back of the room, she began making a fire on

the stone hearth which was set on the floor against the rear wall. Throwing some little piñon branches upon the embers which still smoldered from the morning fire, she stooped and blew until flames started up, while little wisps of smoke curled upward to a vent in the roof. She set a pot of water over the fire, and then stepping through a small doorway into an inner room she began rummaging through the stores for food. She brought out some chunks of deer meat which she threw into the earthen pot, together with a handful of dried beans and some herbs and roots for seasoning. Then, taking a couple of ears of corn, she quickly shelled off the kernels and threw the cobs onto the fire. Squatting down beside a rough stone slab, she took in her hands an oblong stone, and soon there was the satisfying 'huah, huah' of grinding corn.

Before long her son Akoya came in and in a moment a loud 'gautzena' announced the arrival of her noisy, good-natured husband, Zashue. Say began a loud clapping of hands, a welcome sign to her men that she was moulding corn cakes and that supper would soon be ready. She took the steaming pot of stew from the fire and set it before them, then heaped a pile of corn cakes beside it on the earth floor. The father sat cross-legged before this hearty supper, while the boy squatted on his heels and hastily grabbed for the food. His mother stopped him.

'Do not be so greedy, uak' (urchin), she said. 'Remember Those Above.'

Following the example of his parents, Akoya quickly scattered crumbs of sacred meal. Then father and son fell to eating. Folding the corn cakes into a kind of ladle, they dipped out the stew and munched meat and broth and cake together. As each finished, he muttered a 'hoya' of thanksgiving. Zashue and Akoya strolled out together but soon parted, the father making his way to the kiva of his people of the Water clan, while the

Say preparing dinner for her men

son walked toward the kiva of his mother's clan where he had
slept since his thirteenth year.[1]

Say put the supper away by simply dumping the remnants
of the cakes into an earthen bowl and setting the pot in a corner.
She nibbled at one of the cakes, but she was too sick to have
much appetite. Staring out of the doorway as the village settled
itself for the night, she saw the men going down into the kivas,
where they were preparing for the dances which soon would be
given to bring rain.

Darkness settled on the courtyard, lightened somewhat by the

[1] Scholars disagree about the use of kivas among the ancient Pueblos. Today in
the villages of New Mexico the kivas are used by religious societies which are made
up of members of various clans. Bandelier (contrary to some modern scholars)
believed that in old days the kivas were clan houses. In my descriptions of life in
this ancient village I have tried to follow the best modern knowledge. But where
there is dispute (as on this kiva question) I have followed Bandelier.

stars which were so bright in the clear heavens that they seemed to be hanging closer than the jagged turrets that rose in fantastic shapes above the cliff. A little crescent of moon going down at the end of the valley made the trees on the distant mesas look as though they might be enemy Navajos skulking about, ready to pounce upon any of the peaceful village Indians who ventured beyond the protection of their valley. Say shivered and drew her dress more closely about her.

'Gautzena!'

Say started at the sudden greeting, recovering scarcely in time to answer 'opona' (enter), as her companion of the afternoon stepped into the room.

'Where are your men?' asked the visitor.

'My husband is at work with the Delight Makers, who all these nights are making ready for the dance.'

'And the boy?' asked Shuama.

'My son will be with his fellows at our house' (the kiva of the clan).

The two women walked to the back of the room and, sitting on the floor beside the fire, they talked of the day's hunt, of the gossip of the village, of the things women talk of when they sit idling together. Then suddenly Shuama asked Say about her sickness.

'Speak to me,' Shuama said. 'I know many herbs and roots that are good for sickness. I know other things, too,' she whispered. 'It may be I can help you. I was not married to the chief of the Delight Makers for nothing.'

Say shuddered. She knew that Shuama had put out from her house her former husband, Tyope, who was the leader of that band of dancing priests called Koshare or Delight Makers. These men were the sacred clowns. Dressed in grotesque clothes, with painted faces, they romped and tumbled about during the most solemn dances, making the people roar with laughter. Yet they were especially holy; they were supposed to have great power with the spirits. Say had never liked the Koshare with their rough ways. She could not bear their leader who professed holiness and yet was sly in his dealings with his fellows. And she feared that his former wife, who hated him, had learned from him magic secrets which she should not know.

Say was embarrassed by her bold visitor. She did not know her very well, for her clan lived at the far end of the valley, and women worked and visited chiefly with the sisters of their own clan. And while Shuama had always been friendly to her, Say knew that she was not liked in the village. 'A forward woman,' they called her, and sometimes they called her worse. Since the time years ago when she had set the clothes and weapons of Tyope outside their door — notice to him and the village that she was no longer his wife — many young men had offered to share her house. But she had chosen to live alone, and this independence had set her a little apart from the village. While she was always ready to help the other women when they or their children were sick or when a new house was to be plastered or food to be cooked for many guests, the women did not often return her visits. It was reported that she did not always refuse to let men come to her house after the feasts and dances, and it had begun to be whispered that she was a witch, that she kept owl feathers and had even talked with the black corn.

Though Say was fearful of the woman and her reputation, she was calmed by Shuama's gentle words and was slowly led to tell of her illness: how she had burned with fever two winters ago, then had seemed to get well as the dry season came, and had again sickened with the rains. Shuama listened silently, nodding her head.

Speaking slowly, urged on from time to time by her visitor's questions, Say told her story. She had lain for many days weak and hot on the skins in the inner room, while her sisters in the clan had come in to cook for her family. They had fed her tea made from willow bark, and foam made by beating in a pot of water the root of the yucca plant.

When she still shook with fever, medicine men had been called in. Coming at midnight, they had wrapped her in a blanket and carried her to a special curing room, reached by climbing over the roof of a distant house down through a hole in the ceiling to a dark chamber below. Her relatives and friends had followed, huddling at the far side of the chamber, watching as the priests worked to drive out the evil spirits that must be tormenting her. Each priest had brought with him a little image of the Yaya, the mother of all people (a perfect ear of corn wrapped in cotton and buckskin, decked with parrot feathers and adorned with shells). They had held in each hand long eagle feathers with which they brushed her, scooping out the evils from her body and throwing them in the six directions. Then, while the head priest waved a round white stone about his head, his fellows had run out into the night, striking right and left at any evils that might be about, and dashed down to the brook to see if spirits were hiding there. In the end the chief medicine man had put his lips to her body, drawn a great breath, and fallen to the floor as if dead. His assistants had raised him to his feet and helped him as he vomited out the evils he had sucked from her body. Then there was a great feast, and many blue and green stones and buckskin wraps were given to the medicine men. But even this heroic effort did not cure her, for though with the dry weather she got better, she turned sick again with the rains.

Shuama nodded her head slowly and whispered, 'It is as

I thought. You are bewitched by men right here in the pueblo.'

'No!' shouted Say, starting to her feet and shaking with fear and terror more than she had ever shaken with the fever. While witchcraft was regarded as the usual cause of illness, she could not believe that any of her neighbors would want to harm her.

'Yes,' said Shuama. 'I have thought well. Did not your sickness go away in the dry seasons and come again with the rains? And who are the men who bring the rains? Are they not the Koshare, the holy clowns? I know that evil man, Tyope, who is their leader. Did I not live with him for two years? Like the badger for which he is named, he burrows in the darkness, under ground, always scheming some evil.'

'No,' Say whispered, her eyes wide with terror. 'The Delight Makers would not do so vile a thing. What have I done to harm them?'

'Are they precious to you or you to them?' asked Shuama.

'No,' Say admitted. 'They know I do not like them. But my husband is one of them.'

'Your man is good,' said Shuama scornfully, 'but he is like a child. He works in the fields, he hunts, he sits in the kiva, and he is a good and holy clown. But he does not think. Tyope twists him in his hands like dry grass.'

Say knew she was right. Zashue was as thoughtless and playful as a boy.

'You must put a curse back on the Delight Makers,' said Shuama.

'No, no!' cried Say. 'You do not know what you are saying. I will not work against the spirits. Go. Leave me.'

'It is not the spirits we fight,' said Shuama, not moving from the place where she was sitting. 'The Delight Makers have tricked the guardians into wronging you. We must fight that trick with a more powerful curse.'

Say trembled. She was frightened. She knew it was wicked to have any dealings with magic. All that was for the priests. If common people tampered with hidden things they became sorcerers — evil, cursed. But Shuama was a forceful woman. It was not easy to resist her. And as Say sat staring at her, anger at the hideous Delight Makers began to rise against her fear of witchcraft.

Shuama saw the anger in her companion's face. She waited long while the two women said no word. Then very earnestly she whispered, 'Tomorrow night I will bring owl feathers. And you get some ears of black corn. We will see if they will speak to us.'

She was on her feet and out of the doorway before Say could protest. The poor woman sat rigid, too horrified to move. She was still sitting huddled by the dead fire when late that night Zashue returned.

Early next morning Shuama was on the mesa. This was where she loved to be. Her blood tingled as she trod noiselessly through the underbrush. She liked to feel the wind blowing against her limbs as it sighed through the branches of the cedars and shook the bright blue berries that covered the juniper bushes. The wild turkeys flying about the tops of the trees, the rabbits scurrying among the bushes, the coyotes and wildcats padding stealthily through the tangled wood — none of these was more at home on the mesa than she.

She had come on a special errand but she had all day before her. Walking slowly over the rocks and rough ground, she glanced absently about for herbs and roots. But her mission was to find a dead owl whose feathers she could use for the cure of her friend, Say Koitza, and for a curse on her foe, Tyope. She dug up some yucca roots and picked a handful of nuts from the twisted branches of the little piñon trees. Then she saw a dark, ruffled bundle, a dead owl, lying at her feet. Stealthily she kicked it into a dense thicket, noting the place carefully so that she could find it as she came back at the end of the day. No need to run the risk of being met by some man hunting on the mesa who might find on her the evil trophy.

Toward the middle of the day, as she stooped to dig up a root, her elbows were suddenly seized from behind by two strong hands. Terrified, she kept perfectly still, then slowly turned her head and looked up into a face hideous with war paint. She relaxed slowly, and leaning back into strong arms, smiled straight into her captor's face. The man dropped her elbows and jumped away.

Shuama saw at once from his features and dress that the Indian who had captured her was not a Navajo but a member of some village tribe. She knew from his paint and weapons that he was on the warpath. That being the case, he could have no dalliance with women. He might have killed her, but a woman is a poor war trophy. And her lustrous eyes and smiling lips told him he had less than nothing to fear from her.

Standing at a discreet distance, he spoke to her but she could not understand. He pressed his hands against his chest and said over and over, 'Cayamo, Cayamo,' then, pointing far to the north, said, 'Puye, Puye.'

Smiling, she pointed to her breast and answered, 'Shuama, Shuama,' and, waving toward the near-by cliffs, 'Tyuonyi, Tyuonyi.'

They squatted on their heels in the shade of a great cottonwood, still keeping far apart, and talked on in dumb show for many minutes. Shuama knew she was attractive to men and she delighted to play with them. She hugged herself and smiled.

Cayamo was overjoyed. He grinned back through his war paint, pointed to her and to the distant village. Then he began an elaborate pantomime. He laid his head on his hands in token of sleep and held up one finger, then laid his head upon his hands and held up two fingers, then slept again and held up three fingers, continuing until he had counted the five fingers of one hand and three of another. Then he pointed to himself and to his village and laid his head on his hands again, closed his eyes and let out a great snore. At that both laughed loudly.

Shuama knew he meant that at the end of eight sleeps his war path would be ended and he would again be in his village. She went through the whole pantomime as he had done, then pointed to herself and to his village and at the end rested her head softly on her hands and smiled.

The man grinned. He was pleased that he had so skilfully given his meaning. He was taken with this sturdy, handsome woman who seemed so fond of him. Shuama also was glad. He was a strong man and evidently a brave warrior for it is seldom that the peaceful village Indians take the warpath. He was doubtless avenging some evil done to a brother by the fierce Navajos. So he was righteous as well as strong.

She moved toward him but he started back. He pointed to his war signs and shook his head sternly. It was evident that he was no trifler. He knew well the laws of the warpath, and it was clear he meant to obey them. He would touch no woman lovingly until he had fulfilled his revenge and, under the eyes of the priest, had purged himself and scrubbed off his war paint.

Cayamo repeated the series of signs to make sure the woman understood his invitation to his village. Then as she smiled and nodded, he vanished. Where he had stood there was nothing and there was no sound. As she looked down there were no signs on the ground of the direction he had gone. There were scarcely any signs at all, for he wore sandals soled with three hoops of wood on which rabbit skins were bound. The fur made little impression even on soft earth, and if marks were left no one could tell from the hollows made by the three hoops which way the wearer had gone.

Shuama smiled again. He was skilful and stealthy. She had no doubt he would succeed in his revenge and keep himself safe. She had no idea of following him to his home. But she knew that many whispered against her in the village. It was just as well to have a friend to flee to in case of sudden need. And it was always a joy to conquer men.

The sun was almost touching the cliffs over the gorge of Tyuonyi as she walked homeward. Warm with the thought of her new conquest, she did not trouble to be sly in looking for the owl's body hidden in the underbrush. As she stuffed the black feathers into the bosom of her dress she heard a twig snap. She

*Shuama did not trouble to be sly in looking for the
owl's body in the underbrush*

stood rigid, looking carefully about her. She saw nothing and there was no sound. Doubtless Cayamo had followed her and snapped the twig to frighten her, then stolen softly off again.

Shuama could almost see the grin under his daubs of paint as she imagined him chuckling at her fright. What she could not see was the stealthy figure that crept silently away with a grin not of love but of hate — Tyope, who had been hiding all day long in the underbrush of the crags, hoping to surprise his former wife in just such a sin as the gathering of owl feathers.

While Shuama was on the mesa, Say was shaking with fever and fear in her home. She forced herself to clean the house, then went out to join some of her clan sisters who were moulding clay to be burned into pots. Before she left the hut, she had fumbled with trembling hands among the ears of corn stored in the inner room of the hut until she found one with many black kernels. This she thrust inside her dress and kept it there — hidden and burning her guilty breast all day long. She was restless and welcomed the homely tasks with her sisters in the courtyard.

As the sun dipped behind the high cliff, throwing a great shadow over the valley, her son Akoya came home. He was in bad spirits. He had been hunting turkeys on the highlands, but through the long day he had killed no bird. Even a mountain trout which he had caught with his deft hands among the boulders of the little creek — even this had slipped through his fingers just as he was lifting it from the water. And he felt his efforts had not been rewarded because he had forgotten that morning to scatter corn meal in the six sacred directions.

Scarcely had Akoya pushed aside the hide which covered the doorway when Zashue entered also, calling a hearty 'gautzena' to the family. Zashue had been in the fields rooting out weeds from among the maize plants with a wooden knife and helping the men dig a new ditch to carry water from the creek to the gardens. He was tired and hungry and was glad to hear the loud clapping of Say's hands as she moulded corn cakes.

As Zashue waited for his supper, Say looked at him sullenly. She wondered if he could be a party to the curse which his society, the Delight Makers, had put upon her. Then she felt the black corn chafing her skin and turned a guilty, beseeching glance upon her husband.

As the night wore on, after her men had gone to their kivas, Say became more and more nervous. Every instinct rebelled against the rite which Shuama had urged. Clutching the ear of corn, she rose to go to Shuama's house to tell her she would not deal with the black magic. But just then, with a quiet 'gautzena,' the other woman stepped through the doorway. 'Raua' (good), Say whispered in reply, but she knew it was not good. It was all hideous and terrible.

Shuama gave her neighbor no time to protest. Taking Say's trembling hand, she led her to the back of the room. The night was chill, the fire on the hearth was low, only a few embers were still burning. Through the hole that served as the doorway an occasional draught of cold air blew in.

As Shuama went stolidly about her ritual, Say clung to her shoulder, shivering from cold and fear. In the center of the dark room Shuama placed in two bundles the owl's feathers that she had gathered that day on the mesa. She took the ear of corn from Say and broke a dozen black kernels onto the floor beside the feathers. She took some bark of red willow that she had brought from her store of medicines, and, grinding it in her hands, rolled it within corn husks to make two crude cigarettes. Handing one of these to Say, she told her to light it from the embers, puff the smoke in the six sacred directions, and cast the glowing stub on the pile of corn and feathers. With a shudder Say obeyed, her teeth chattering while the woman recited an incantation. Then both huddled together to listen. Even Shuama felt afraid. Everything was silent; the cold draught from the outside had stopped; the women sat breathless; they listened and listened. Nothing moved; there was not a sound.

Shuama swallowed her fear, gave a second cigarette to Say, and repeated the dread formula. Suddenly a cold blast whispered through the room. It fanned the embers to renewed life; there was a glimmer, a crackling; the feathers moved; the grains of corn seemed to change position. One of the feather bunches rolled on the floor. Ghostly whispers filled the air. The women stifled screams of terror. The black corn had spoken.

Say fainted. Her neighbor carried her into the inner room where she lay in fitful sleep. Shuama stole back to the hearth and, digging in the ground of the floor with a stone knife, she buried the owl feathers and corn, making the earth smooth and hard over the hidden omens by packing it carefully with her hands and stamping it firm and level with her bare feet. The omens must be left in the home to complete the cure. Later she would bury them elsewhere as a curse against Tyope. Quietly she went out of the house and walked through the sleeping village to her cave among the Water people.

As she walked away she did not see the figure hiding in the shadow — Tyope, whose little badger eyes had been keeping vigil at Say's doorway. He had not been able to see what went on behind the deerskin within the dark room but the stealthy actions of the women told the story. He had evidence enough from seeing Shuama with the owl feathers on the mesa to convict her before the village council and have her killed as a witch. With a little more proof he could ruin Say Koitza also — Say who looked through him as if he were not there. He rubbed his tongue over his lips and pressed his hands strongly against his chest as he tasted his revenge and thought how honor would come to him as the guardian of village morals.

When Say awoke from troubled sleep in the middle of the night, Zashue was snoring rhythmically by her side. She started up, crept into the kitchen, and fumbled blindly around for the dread omens. There was nothing. With a glad sigh, she realized that her friend had taken care to hide all signs of their terrible deed. She stole back to her husband's side and stretched herself out on the hides beside him.

For days thereafter, whenever Zashue approached her, Say had a guilty pang. She was an evil woman, she felt, unworthy of the bantering jokes and clumsy caresses of her husband. She shuddered away from his touch as she remembered that it was against the Delight Makers, the society of which he was so joyous a member, that the magic had been worked. Every time she cooked the simple meals for her household, she seemed to see beneath the hearth the terrible feathers of the owl, the ugly black kernels of corn. But steadily she got better and stronger. Maybe the hideous rite had removed the curse from her without any injury to the Koshare.

One afternoon, in the slow sequence of days that made up the life of the village, an old man climbed the notched pole that led to the terrace on which Say's house stood. With firm step he approached her door. Akoya, sitting outside, looked up in surprise to see the martial figure.

'Yaya, sa umo' (mother, my grandfather), he called.

The old man nodded to the handsome youth, bent his tall, straight body, and stepped through the low doorway. He stood just inside the room and fixed his gaze on Say. He was Topanashka, the Masewi, the war chief of the village, feared and respected for his skill and bravery and for his stern virtue and obedience to the traditions of the tribe. Say was his daughter.

She had been his only child, and there was deep affection between the two, though they had seen little of each other during
all the years that Say had had a husband in her house and
Topanashka had taken on the solemn duties of war captain.

'Child,' the old man said, 'where is your husband?'

'Zashue Tihua (the man Zashue) is in the fields.'

'When will he come?'

The woman raised her hand, pointed to the hole in the wall,
and then made a sign of blotting out the light by way of saying
that her husband would not return until the sun ceased to shine
through the hole.

'Raua,' the man said. 'I would talk.'

There was a long silence. At last, looking sternly at her, he
said, 'Is it true that you have listened to the black corn?'

'Who says so?' demanded the woman.

'The Delight Makers,' answered her father.

'What do I care for them?' the woman asked angrily.

'It may be that you do not hold them precious. But I know
that they watch you.'

'Let them do as they please. I am a good woman. I live with
my husband. I cook for my family. I attend the ceremonies.'

'Woman,' the old man said sternly, 'you have been good, but
people say now that your ways are black. The Delight Makers
know it; they know much more than I wish.'

Long the two sat in silence.

'Have the Delight Makers sent you to me?' she asked in de-
spair.

'No,' said her father, 'but if they speak against you and the
old men of the council come to me and say "kill the witch" I
must do it. I am Masewi; I do what the principals advise.'

The woman bowed her head, staring straight at the floor

beneath her. After many minutes, while the man stood gravely before her, she raised her eyes a little and spoke.

'Umo,' she said, 'are those who are precious to the holders of our path, are they always good? Do the holy clowns do no evil?'

'I need not speak to you about such things,' the old man said sternly. Then, relenting a little, he spoke on. 'Sa uishe' (my child), he said, 'I will say to you that men speak evil of the chief of the holy clowns. Good men say Tyope seeks always to puff himself up.' Then, hesitantly, 'You must take care. There are whispers that he creeps about the mesa watching the witch gather owl feathers.'

Say started. Then Tyope had spied on Shuama. That was how their guilty secret had leaked out. She shivered as she pictured the Badger whispering his suspicions, not daring to make a formal charge to the council until he had inflamed the village against the witches. She said nothing.

Topanashka stiffened. 'I need not speak to you of such things,' he said harshly. Then he turned, stooped through the doorway, and strode away.

Left alone, the woman drew her hair over her face and wept. Alone she cowered among the ashes. Loneliness, she thought, rocking back and forth in her grief, had always been with her. Even in childhood she had been lonely; there had been no brothers and sisters to play with, and only a deaf mother for company. Even when Zashue had come courting, Say had had to make her decision by herself, for she could not shriek of such delicate matters to her deaf mother, and her father was not only stern but, being a member of another clan, he could not properly take any part in the marriage of his daughter, which was chiefly a clan affair. As she sat sobbing she thought of her courtship in those days long ago.

As a girl of fourteen she had first noticed the gay, handsome youth, Zashue. He called often at her home. And one morning when she was climbing up the hillside from the brook, a jar filled with water on her head, he stopped her, dipped some water from the urn to drink, and whispered that he would bring her a buckskin. She gave no reply but ran scurrying home to ponder alone all day. Then, taking a tray of corn cakes, she climbed the jagged slope to the highest dwellings of the Water clan to which Zashue belonged. The lad was sitting in his family's cave, straightening some arrow shafts over the fire, when the girl, pushing the tray before her, crept through the hole. Silently she placed the food before his mother and went out without a word. With his proposal thus formally accepted, Zashue visited the quarters of the Gourd people every night.

It all seemed so far away to Say. Now she was alone, more than she had ever been, for her husband, boisterous and gay, was no companion with whom she could share her thoughts and cares. Her father had withdrawn more and more as village duties kept him busy. Her mother had died soon after her marriage, of a fever — maybe the same fever that was now wracking Say's frail body. When Akoya had been small he was company for her, but now he was grown and cared no more for the society of his mother. If only the little ones who came after Akoya had lived, they would have been some comfort in her loneliness. But these too had gone from her. Today she needed a friend as never before, and the only friend she could count on was a witch.

Next day the sun rose bright and clear. The air was so dry that in spite of her terror Say felt almost cured of her fever. The sky was so blue, the wind so brisk, that Say gathered together the few clothes of her family and took them down to the little stream where she rubbed them with yucca roots to loosen the dirt, beat them with rocks, and rinsed them in the clear brook.

It was the day of the dance of the Delight Makers. And Say had scarcely got back to her home from her washing before the festival started. The dancing society was using the plaza within the great amphitheatre of which her own home was a part. Standing by her doorway, Say had a fine view of the ceremony. Caught up in the rhythm and pageantry, she pushed aside her worries.

Hu-hu! Hu-hu! Hu-hu! Hu-o-o-o-o!

The final whoop, caught up by the cliffs of Tyuonyi, echoed and re-echoed in a prolonged howl. The dancers marched into the courtyard and the chorus grew louder as it burst into the refrain.

Ho a a! Heiti-na! Ho-a-a! Heiti-na!

The procession danced about the plaza in a double column, men on one side and women on the other, the men stamping out the measure, the women tripping lightly in a double step.

The men wore kilts, made of cotton cloth or deerskin, which hung from the waist and flapped about the knees. Tortoise-shell rattles and clattering clusters of elk hoofs dangled from tight belts of red and yellow buckskin bound below each knee. About the ankles were strips of white and black fur from the skunk. Fox skins hung down their backs like great tails. Their long black hair hung loose, and tufts of green and yellow feathers fluttered over their foreheads. About their necks and naked chests were strings of shell beads, turquoises, bright stones. In their hands they carried tufts of hawk feathers and rattles made of gourds and pebbles. Their faces and naked torsos were daubed with white paint.

The women wore their ordinary dress, for in this dance the Indians say the men are the stars, the women the dark spaces between the stars. But even the women's work-a-day dresses were brightened by necklaces, wrist bands, and ear pendants.

The Delight Makers tumbled into the court

In each hand they carried a bunch of spruce boughs which they swished from side to side as they danced and chanted.

Stomping and shouting, the great double column marched about the court as a chorus of old men sang and a drummer beat monotonously on a hollow log covered at each end with taut rawhide. Suddenly the beat of the drum stopped and the procession broke into chattering, laughing, panting groups. Then peals of laughter shook the crowd. The clowns were coming.

Half a dozen men tumbled into the court, hopping, running, cutting clumsy capers, while the spectators applauded with shouts and guffaws. The bodies of these clowns, streaked with white paint, were naked, save for tattered breechcloths; their hair was gathered in topknots from which waved bunches of corn husks; their mouths and eyes were circled with rings of black paint. These jesters were the sacred clowns. They had charge of the ripening of the corn and of the children growing

As the procession broke into chattering groups

within the women's wombs. While their role in the dance was buffoonery, the holy clowns were among the most feared and honored of the shamans of the tribe.

Rushing about the courtyard, climbing over the roofs of the houses, tumbling off ladders, the clowns convulsed the spectators with loud laughter. Two of them, pairing off, mocked the dance that had just ended, one stomping with high awkward steps, the other mincing and tripping in burlesque of the women dancers. One rolled in the dirt while another grabbed his legs and dragged him through the dust to the guffaws of the crowd. One jumped onto a roof and scattered the girls with his coarse jibes and coarser gestures. Others rushed into one of the houses, overturned everything, and brought out skins and pots which they dashed to pieces on the ground, while the owners looked on wistfully and their neighbors howled with laughter.

As the buffoonery subsided and the drum started up for

another dance, Say's father, who had been watching the antics from a near-by roof, walked slowly past her. Without stopping or glancing at her, he whispered, 'Get the owl feathers before the Delight Makers find them.'

Say, who had almost forgotten her terror in watching the dance and laughing at the clowns, stood rigid until the old man had passed on. She remembered that the house next door had been torn up. If the Delight Makers suspected her, how easy for them to raid her house, turn everything upside down, even tear up the earth floor until they found the telltale feathers of the owl and the damning kernels of black corn. Quickly she shuffled into her house. She had no fear of being seen, for everyone was outside watching the dance. If only she could get the feathers before the Koshare began their games again.

Her fingers tore at the hard earth. She seized a stick from the pile of firewood and dug into the floor. It seemed minutes — hours — until the stick at last struck a soft, resisting mass. Hastily she thrust in her hand, felt around for every feather and every grain of corn, and crammed the whole cursed mass into the pouch formed by the bosom of her dress. In a frenzy she scraped the earth back, tamped it down hard and smooth with her feet, and scattered ashes about to hide any signs of her digging. Shaking, almost fainting with haste and fear, she walked to the door and stolidly took up her stand again by the wall of her house.

Just in time. For as she leaned her trembling body against the hot adobe wall, another shout went up and the clowns began again their revels. At once two fierce-looking jesters dashed across the courtyard and into her doorway, shouting and hurling out skins and mats as they climbed in. She knew them through their garish paint. She shuddered at the sight of Tyope, chief of the Koshare band. Her heart stopped as in the other she saw